Writers
on
Writing

By the Same Author

The Portable Curmudgeon

♦

Zen to Go

♦

A Curmudgeon's Garden of Love

♦

Friendly Advice

Writers
on
Writing

SELECTED
AND
COMPILED
BY

JON WINOKUR

RUNNING PRESS • PHILADELPHIA
PENNSYLVANIA

Canadian representatives: General Publishing Co., Ltd., 30 Lesmill Road,
Don Mills, Ontario M3B 2T6. International representatives: Worldwide Media
Services, Inc., 115 East Twenty-third Street, New York, New York 10010.

Library of Congress Cataloging in Publication Data:
Writers on writing.
Includes index.
    1. Authorship—Quotations, maxims, etc.   2. Authors—Quotations.
        I. Winokur, Jon
ISBN 0-89471-877-0

Printed in the United States by Bertelsmann Printing and Manufacturing

Cover design by Toby Schmidt
Interior design and layout by Dennis Roberts
Illustrations by Charles Dougherty
Typography: Palacio by Commcor Communications Corporation,
Philadelphia, Pennsylvania; Phyllis and Phyllis by Letraset.

Running Press Book Publishers
125 South Twenty-second Street
Philadelphia, Pennsylvania 19103

For Skip and Elinor

*Table
of
Contents*

Acknowledgments

I'm grateful to Lawrence Teacher and Stuart Teacher of
Running Press for their extraordinary commitment to this book.
I wish to thank Nanette Bendyna, Melissa Cookman,
Charles Dougherty, Dorothy Hoffman, Cynthia Johnson,
Nancy Lea Johnson, Howard LeNoble, Anita Nelson,
Susan Nethery, Dennis Roberts, Toby Schmidt, Laurie Schlesinger,
Steve Schuhle, Nancy Steele, Frank Zachary, Steve Zorn,
and Elizabeth Zozom for their invaluable help.
I'm indebted to Tobi Sanders, Linda Takahashi,
and Mark Wolgin for their support and good counsel.

Introduction

I love quotations. Maybe it's a symptom of a short-attention-span, instant-gratification age, but I'm a sucker for a well stated tidbit of brevity and wit. For me, quotes do with precision what reading does in general: they confirm the astuteness of my perceptions, they open the way to ideas, and they console me with the knowledge that I'm not alone.

I began collecting quotes on writing at the age of seventeen, when I first had the notion to be a writer. I was fascinated with the creative process and curious about writing as an occupation. I wanted to know why and how and when and where they do it. I wanted to know what it *takes* to be a writer.

Fortunately, most writers love to talk about it.

They're full of advice to young writers, prescriptions for success and failure, and tips on dealing with demon publishers. They philosophize about Art and posit definitions of Style. They have opinions on censorship, plagiarism, and the need to revise. They speculate on the role of alcohol in the production of literature and declare why they write. They divulge trade secrets such as how to plan a novel and how to handle an editor. They gossip about colleagues and grapple with the terror of the blank page. They lament the agony of rejection. They feel guilty when they don't write. They discuss their characters as if they were real people, and they get even with critics.

They talk about talking about writing.

And above all, they display their talent, dedication and humanity.

Here, then, the result of twenty years of compulsive collecting, to be read for amusement, for reference, or out of sheer fascination with the writer's art.

Advice to Young Writers

He that will write well in any tongue must follow this counsel of Aristotle: to speak as the common people do, to think as wise men do.

Roger Ascham

♦

Take care of the sense and the sounds will take care of themselves.

Lewis Carroll

♦

Be born anywhere, little embryo novelist, but do not be born under the shadow of a great creed, not under the burden of original sin, not under the doom of salvation.

Pearl S. Buck

It is by sitting down to write every morning that one becomes a writer. Those who do not do this remain amateurs.

Gerald Brenan

♦

A writer shouldn't be engaged with other writers, or with people who make books, or even with people who read them. The farther away you get from the literary traffic, the closer you are to sources. I mean, a writer doesn't really *live*, he observes.

Nelson Algren

♦

There is only one place to write and that is *alone* at a typewriter. The writer who has to go *into* the streets is a writer who does not know the streets. . .*when you leave your typewriter you leave your machine gun and the rats come pouring through.*

Charles Bukowski

♦

For Godsake, keep your *eyes* open. Notice what's going on around you.

William Burroughs

Writing has laws of perspective, of light and shade, just as painting does, or music. If you are born knowing them, fine. If not, learn them. Then rearrange the rules to suit yourself.

Truman Capote

♦

It's not wise to violate the rules until you know how to observe them.

T.S. Eliot

♦

The discipline of the writer is to learn to be still and listen to what his subject has to tell him.

Rachel Carson

♦

You write a hit play the same way you write a flop.

William Saroyan

♦

To a chemist, nothing on earth is unclean. A writer must be as objective as a chemist; he must abandon the subjective line; he must know that dungheaps play a very respectable part in a landscape, and that evil passions are as inherent in life as good ones.

Anton Chekov

Never demean yourself by talking back to a critic, never.
Write those letters to the editor in your head, but don't put
them on paper.

Truman Capote

♦

Listen carefully to first criticisms of your work. Note just what
it is about your work the critics don't like—then cultivate it.
That's the part of your work that's individual and worth
keeping.

Jean Cocteau

♦

I would recommend the cultivation of extreme indifference
to both praise and blame because praise will lead you to vanity, and blame will lead you to self-pity, and both are bad
for writers.

John Berryman

♦

For god's sake, don't do it unless you have to. . .It's not easy.
It shouldn't be easy, but it shouldn't be impossible, and it's
damn near impossible.

Frank Conroy

If a young writer can refrain from writing, he shouldn't hesitate to do so.

André Gide

♦

The main suggestion from me is *read*. It is impossible for a writer to be able to write honestly and eloquently without having at one time or another acquainted himself with such writers as Sir Thomas Browne.

William Styron

♦

Read as many of the great books as you can before the age of 22.

James Michener

♦

Read, read, read. Read everything—trash, classics, good and bad, and see how they do it. Just like a carpenter who works as an apprentice and studies the master. Read! You'll absorb it. Then write. If it is good, you'll find out. If it's not, throw it out the window.

William Faulkner

♦

If you would be a reader, read; if a writer, write.

Epictetus

If you want to be true to life, start lying about it.

John Fowles

♦

Writing is easy; all you do is sit staring at a blank sheet of paper until the drops of blood form on your forehead.

Gene Fowler

♦

There's nothing to writing. All you do is sit down at a typewriter and open a vein.

Red Smith

♦

Nothing you write, if you hope to be any good, will ever come out as you first hoped.

Lillian Hellman

♦

Never write about a place until you're away from it, because it gives you perspective. Immediately after you've seen something you can give a photographic description of it and make it accurate. That's good practice, but it isn't creative writing.

Ernest Hemingway

The last paragraph in which you tell what the story is about is almost always best left out.

Irwin Shaw

♦

Read over your compositions and, when you meet a passage which you think is particularly fine, strike it out.

Samuel Johnson

♦

Let your literary compositions be kept from the public eye for nine years at least.

Horace

♦

One should never write down or up to people, but out of yourself.

Christopher Isherwood

♦

Word-carpentry is like any other kind of carpentry: you must join your sentences smoothly.

Anatole France

♦

Only ambitious nonentities and hearty mediocrities exhibit their rough drafts. It is like passing around samples of one's sputum.

Vladimir Nabokov

A good many young writers make the mistake of enclosing a stamped, self-addressed envelope, big enough for the manuscript to come back in. That is too much of a temptation to the editor.

Ring Lardner

◆

Never submit an idea or chapter to an editor or publisher, no matter how much he would like you to. . . . This is your story. Try and find out what your editor wants in advance, but then try and give it to him in one piece.

John Creasey

◆

It's not a good idea to try to put your wife into a novel. . .not your latest wife anyway.

Norman Mailer

◆

Writing is a wholetime job: no professional writer can afford only to write when he feels like it.

W. Somerset Maugham

◆

Get black on white.

Guy de Maupassant

Vladimir Nabokov

(1899–1977)

Beware the modish message. Ask yourself if the symbol you have detected is not your own footprint.

Oh, shun, lad, the life of an author.
  It's nothing but worry and waste.
Avoid that utensil,
The laboring pencil,
  And pick up the scissors and paste.

Phyllis McGinley

◆

Everyone who does not *need* to be a writer, who thinks he can do something else, ought to do something else.

Georges Simenon

◆

First of all, you must have an agent, and in order to get a good one, you must have sold a considerable amount of material. And in order to sell a considerable amount of material, you must have an agent. Well, you get the idea.

Steve McNeil

◆

Once you start illustrating virtue as such you had better stop writing fiction. Do something else, like Y-work. Or join a committee. Your business as a writer is not to illustrate virtue, but to show how a fellow may move toward it—or away from it.

Robert Penn Warren

Unless you think you can do better than Tolstoy, we don't need you.

James Michener

♦

If you're going to write, don't pretend to write down. It's going to be the best you can do, and it's the fact that it's the best you can do that kills you!

Dorothy Parker

♦

Lay off the muses, it's a very tough dollar.

S.J. Perelman

♦

The secret of popular writing is never to put more on a given page than the common reader can lap off it with no strain WHATSOEVER on his habitually slack attention.

Ezra Pound

♦

Never make excuses, never let them see you bleed, and never get separated from your baggage.

Wesley Price

♦

Better to write for yourself and have no public, than write for the public and have no self.

Cyril Connolly

If you want to get rich from writing, write the sort of thing that's read by persons who move their lips when they're reading to themselves.

Don Marquis

♦

Keep going. Writing is finally play, and there's no reason why you should get paid for playing. If you're a real writer, you'll write no matter what.

Irwin Shaw

♦

You can't want to be a writer, you have to *be* one.

Paul Theroux

♦

In composing, as a general rule, run your pen through every other word you have written; you have no idea what vigor it will give to your style.

Sydney Smith

♦

Write freely and as rapidly as possible and throw the whole thing on paper. Never correct or rewrite until the whole thing is down. Rewrite in process is usually found to be an excuse for not going on.

John Steinbeck

Advice to young writers who want to get ahead without any annoying delays: don't write about Man, write about a man.

E.B. White

♦

The idea is to get the pencil moving quickly.

Bernard Malamud

♦

Blot out, correct, insert, refine,
Enlarge, diminish, interline;
Be mindful, when invention fails,
To scratch your head, and bite your nails.

Jonathan Swift

♦

Not that the story need be long, but it will take a long while to make it short.

Henry David Thoreau

♦

If you are in difficulties with a book, try the element of surprise: attack it at an hour when it isn't expecting it.

H.G. Wells

With the pride of the artist, you must blow against the walls
of every power that exists, the small trumpet of your defiance.
Norman Mailer

◆

Be obscure clearly.

E.B. White

◆

Authors—essayist, atheist, novelist,
    realist, rhymster, play your part,
Paint the mortal shame of nature
    with living hues of Art.
Rip your brothers' vices open, strip
    your own foul passions bare;
Down with Reticence, down with Reverence—
    forward—naked—let them stare.

Alfred, Lord Tennyson

◆

Write your heart out.

Bernard Malamud

◆

As to the adjective: when in doubt, strike it out.
Mark Twain

Nice writing isn't enough. It isn't enough to have smooth and pretty language. You have to surprise the reader frequently, you can't just be nice all the time. Provoke the reader. Astonish the reader. Writing that has no surprises is as bland as oatmeal. Surprise the reader with the unexpected verb or adjective. Use one startling adjective per page.

Anne Bernays

♦

If you can tell stories, create characters, devise incidents, and have sincerity and passion, it doesn't matter a damn how you write.

W. Somerset Maugham

♦

There is no advice to give young poets.

Pablo Neruda

♦

If I had to give young writers advice, I'd say don't listen to writers talking about writing or themselves.

Lillian Hellman

Angst

Suffering is the main condition of the artistic experience.
Samuel Beckett

♦

Fear ringed by doubt is my eternal moon.

Malcolm Lowry

♦

Loneliness is your companion for life. If you don't want to be lonely, you get into TV.

William Styron

♦

Every creator painfully experiences the chasm between his inner vision and its ultimate expression. The chasm is never completely bridged. We all have the conviction, perhaps illusory, that we have much more to say than appears on the paper.

Isaac Bashevis Singer

I am profoundly uncertain about how to write. I know what I love or what I like, because it's a direct, passionate response. But when I write I'm very uncertain whether it's good enough. That is, of course, the writer's agony.

Susan Sontag

♦

I find writing very nervous work. I'm always in a dither when starting a novel—that's the worst time. It's like going to the dentist, because you do make a kind of appointment with yourself.

Kingsley Amis

♦

All art is a kind of confession, more or less oblique. All artists, if they are to survive, are forced, at last, to tell the whole story; to vomit the anguish up.

James Baldwin

♦

If I feel it, I feel it now and then, but I don't try to cherish it nor do I feel especially proud of it. It comes on me, let's say, as a headache or toothache might come, and I do my best to discourage it.

Jorge Luis Borges

I have cultivated my hysteria with joy and terror.
Charles Baudelaire

◆

Writing is not a profession but a vocation of unhappiness.
I don't think an artist can ever be happy.
Georges Simenon

◆

Writing is pretty crummy on the nerves.
Paul Theroux

◆

It's a nauseous process.
Rebecca West

◆

Let's face it, writing is hell.
William Styron

◆

Writing is so difficult that I often feel that writers, having
had their hell on earth, will escape all punishment hereafter.
Jessamyn West

◆

I'm not happy when I'm writing, but I'm more unhappy
when I'm not.
Fannie Hurst

Who casts to write a living line, must sweat.

Ben Jonson

♦

Writing is the diametric opposite of having fun. All of life, as far as I'm concerned, is an excuse not to write. I just write when fear overtakes me. It causes paralytic terror. It's really scary just getting to the desk—we're talking now five hours. My mouth gets dry, my heart beats fast. I react psychologically the way other people react when the plane loses an engine.

Fran Lebowitz

♦

It's a very excruciating life facing that blank piece of paper every day and having to reach up somewhere into the clouds and bring something down out of them.

Truman Capote

♦

When you're writing, that's when you're lonely. I suppose that gets into the characters you're writing about. There are hours and hours of silence.

Dick Francis

I used to greet each morning spitting blood in the washbasin, having the night before gnashed the inside of my mouth while dreaming I had misplaced a comma in my writing of that day, throwing off the pattern of speech given to a character who lived two hundred years ago. Years later a dentist asked me if I had a history of mental illness, because the mentally ill often exhibit the advanced molar grindings I did.

Thomas Sanchez

♦

You have to sink way down to a level of hopelessness and desperation to find the book that you can write.

Susan Sontag

♦

You can lie to your wife or your boss, but you cannot lie to your typewriter. Sooner or later you must reveal your true self in your pages.

Leon Uris

♦

When God hands you a gift, he also hands you a whip; and the whip is intended solely for self-flagellation.

Truman Capote

Ernest Hemingway

(1899–1961)

I like to do and can do many things better than I can write, but when I don't write, I feel like shit. I've got the talent and I feel that I'm wasting it.

The malaise of writing—and it is of no consequence whether the writer is talented or otherwise—is that after a time a man writing arrives at a point outside human relationships, becomes, as it were, ahuman.

Frederick Exley

◆

I do not understand this chronic illness. I wish I had gone to law school.

Darryl Pinckney

Art and the Artist

I feel that art has something to do with the achievement of stillness in the midst of chaos. A stillness which characterizes prayer, too, and the eye of the storm. I think that art has something to do with an arrest of attention in the midst of distraction.

Saul Bellow

◆

Art is a vision of heaven gratuitously given.

Anthony Burgess

◆

Art is nature speeded up and God slowed down.

Malcolm De Chazal

◆

Art is life seen through a temperament.

Émile Zola

All art is a struggle to be, in a particular sort of way, virtuous.

Iris Murdoch

♦

All art is a revolt against man's fate.

André Malraux

♦

Art is the apotheosis of solitude.

Samuel Beckett

♦

Art is an attempt to integrate evil.

Simone de Beauvoir

♦

Art never initiates. It merely takes over what is already present in the real world and makes an aesthetic pattern out of it, or tries to explain it, or tries to relate it to some other aspect of life.

Anthony Burgess

♦

The difference between Art and Life is that Art is more bearable.

Charles Bukowski

We have art in order not to die of the truth.
Friedrich Wilhelm Nietzsche

♦

Art, like morality, consists in drawing the line somewhere.
G.K. Chesterton

♦

The containment of our confusions is what we call sanity. The resolution of confusions, the painstaking removal of the stew's ingredients and the remaking of a better stew is what we call art.

Geoffrey Wolff

♦

Art is a marriage of the conscious and the unconscious.
Jean Cocteau

♦

A work that aspires, however humbly, to the condition of art should carry its justification in every line.

Joseph Conrad

♦

A tale charms by its ingenuity, by the plausibility with which it overcomes the suspicion that it couldn't happen. That is art.
Jacques Barzun

To make us feel small in the right way is a function of art. Men can only make us feel small in the wrong way.

E.M. Forster

◆

The work of art is an idea that one exaggerates.

André Gide

◆

A great work of art is a kind of suicide.

Al Alvarez

◆

Art is uncompromising, and life is full of compromises.

Günter Grass

◆

Art-speech is the only truth. An artist is usually a damned liar, but his art, if it be art, will tell you the truth of his day.

D.H. Lawrence

◆

Art for art's sake makes no more sense than gin for gin's sake.

W. Somerset Maugham

Art is only a means to life, to the life more abundant. It merely points the way.

Henry Miller

♦

A work of art has no importance whatever to society. It is only important to the individual.

Vladimir Nabokov

♦

It is the function of art to renew our perception. What we are familiar with we cease to see. The writer shakes up the familiar scene, and as if by magic, we see a new meaning in it.

Anaïs Nin

♦

Art is a form of catharsis.

Dorothy Parker

♦

Art is the reasoned derangement of the senses.

Kenneth Rexroth

In everything that can be called art there is a quality of redemption. It may be pure tragedy, if it is high tragedy, and it may be pity and irony, and it may be the raucous laughter of the strong man. But down these mean streets a man must go who is not himself mean, who is neither tarnished nor afraid. The detective in this kind of story must be such a man.

Raymond Chandler

♦

Art must take reality by surprise.

Françoise Sagan

♦

Art is like a border of flowers along the course of civilization.
Lincoln Steffens

♦

Without art, the crudeness of reality would make the world unbearable.

George Bernard Shaw

♦

Without freedom, no art; art lives only on the restraint it imposes on itself, and dies of all others.

Albert Camus

Art is simpler than people think because there is so little to write about. All the moving things are eternal in man's history and have been written before, and if a man writes hard enough, sincerely enough, and with the unalterable determination never, never to be quite satisfied with it he will repeat them because art, like poverty, takes care of its own, shares its bread.

William Faulkner

♦

A work of art is not a matter of thinking beautiful thoughts or experiencing tender emotions (though those are its raw materials) but of intelligence, skill, taste, proportion, knowledge, discipline and industry; especially discipline.

Evelyn Waugh

♦

Emotion resulting from a work of art is only of value when it is not obtained by sentimental blackmail.

Jean Cocteau

♦

All art has this characteristic—it unites people.

Leo Tolstoy

♦

All good art is indiscretion.

Tennessee Williams

My first thought about art, as a child, was that the artist brings something into the world that didn't exist before, and that he does it without destroying something else. A kind of refutation of the conservation of matter. That still seems to me its central magic, its core of joy.

John Updike

◆

The artist is of no importance. Only what he creates is important, since there is nothing new to be said.

William Faulkner

◆

Artists can color the sky red because they know it's blue. Those of us who aren't artists must color things the way they really are or people might think we're stupid.

Jules Feiffer

◆

The vanity of the artist is of a very curious nature because it is tied to death. Trying to cheat it. And all perfect nonsense, but it fills the days.

Gore Vidal

◆

An artist must be a reactionary. He has to stand out against the tenor of the age and not go flopping along.

Evelyn Waugh

You can only be an artist if you've been up to a point lucky with your background and put in years of reading; you can't step off the factory conveyor-belt and do it.

Martin Amis

♦

All artists are two-headed calves.

Truman Capote

♦

The true artist declares himself by leaving out a lot. The artist alone sees spirits. But after he has told of their appearing to him, everybody sees them.

Goethe

♦

The artist, like the God of creation, remains within or behind or beyond or above his handiwork, invisible, refined, out of existence, indifferent, paring his fingernails.

James Joyce

♦

The better the artist, the more vulnerable he seems to be.

Al Alvarez

♦

When those old writing boys get to talking about The Artist, meaning themselves, I want to leave the profession.

John Steinbeck

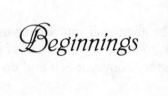

Beginnings

I always begin with a character, or characters, and then try to think up as much action for them as possible.

John Irving

♦

With me, a story usually begins with a single idea or memory or mental picture. The writing of the story is simply a matter of working up to that moment, to explain why it happened or what caused it to follow.

William Faulkner

♦

All my books literally come to me in the form of a sentence, an original sentence which contains the entire book.

Raymond Federman

I know very dimly when I start what's going to happen. I just have a very general idea, and then the thing develops as I write.

Aldous Huxley

♦

I try to know as much as I can about a book before the beginning, but I never know exactly where it's going to end.

Scott Spencer

♦

I've never outlined a novel before starting to write it—at the outset I've never been aware of the story I was trying to handle except in the most general terms. The beginnings of my novels have always been mere flickerings in the imagination, though in each case the flickerings have been generated, clearly enough, by a kind of emotional ferment that had been in process for some time.

John Hawkes

♦

I don't see how anybody starts a novel without knowing how it's going to end. I usually make detailed outlines: how many chapters it will be and so forth.

John Barth

I always start writing with a clean piece of paper and a dirty mind.

Patrick Dennis

♦

You don't start with any aesthetic manifesto, you just do what works.

E.L. Doctorow

♦

Beginning a book is unpleasant. I'm entirely uncertain about the character and the predicament, and a character in his predicament is what I have to begin with. Worse than not knowing your subject is not knowing how to treat it, because that's finally everything. I type out beginnings and they're awful, more of an unconscious parody of my previous book than the breakaway from it that I want. I need something driving down the center of a book, a magnet to draw everything to it—that's what I look for during the first months of writing something new.

Philip Roth

♦

The beginning of a novel is a time of awful torment, when you're dealing with a lot of dead pieces and you have to wait and wait for some kind of animation.

Iris Murdoch

I start at the beginning, go on to the end, then stop.

Anthony Burgess

♦

You think about what actually happened, you tell friends long stories about it, you mull it over in your mind, you connect it together at leisure, then when the time comes to pay the rent again you force yourself to sit at the typewriter, or at the writing notebook, and get it over with as fast as you can.

Jack Kerouac

♦

I always know the ending; that's where I start.

Toni Morrison

♦

I start with a tingle, a kind of feeling of the story I will write. Then come the characters, and they take over, they make the story.

Isak Dinesen

♦

I always have at the very start a curiously clear preview of the entire novel before me or above me.

Vladimir Nabokov

Sometimes you get a line, a phrase, sometimes you're crying, or it's the curve of a chair that hurts you and you don't know why, or sometimes you just want to write a poem, and you don't know what it's about. I will fool around on the typewriter. It might take me ten pages of nothing, of terrible writing, and then I'll get a line, and I'll think, "That's what I mean!" What you're doing is hunting for what you mean, what you're trying to say. You don't know when you start.

Anne Sexton

◆

I usually spend a very long time thinking about it. Sometimes years. You know when you are able to write it. The work goes in before you start, really. You can have variations of the pattern, but the whole book must be there.

Doris Lessing

◆

When I write poetry, what I really get first is one or two phrases with a very insistent rhythm. The phrases keep insisting and the poem builds up by a process of accretion.

Kenneth Rexroth

◆

Usually I begin a poem with an image or phrase; if you follow trustfully, it's surprising how far an image can lead.

James Merrill

If I didn't know the ending of a story, I wouldn't begin. I always write my last line, my last paragraphs, my last page first.
Katherine Anne Porter

♦

The last thing we decide in writing a book is what to put first.
Blaise Pascal

Best-Sellers

A best-seller is the gilded tomb of a mediocre talent.
Logan Pearsall Smith

♦

Best-Sellerism is the star system of the book world. A "best-seller" is a celebrity among books. It is known primarily (sometimes exclusively) for its well-knownness.
Daniel J. Boorstin

♦

Can anybody be so naive as to think he or she can learn anything about the past from those buxom best-sellers that are hawked around by book clubs under the heading of historical novels?
Vladimir Nabokov

The writing of a best-seller represents only a fraction of the total effort required to create one.

Ted Nicholas

◆

If we should ever inaugurate a hall of fame, it would be reserved exclusively and hopefully for authors who, having written four best-sellers, *still refrained* from starting out on a lecture tour.

E.B. White

◆

A best-seller was a book which somehow sold well simply because it was selling well.

Daniel J. Boorstin

◆

The principle of procrastinated rape is said to be the ruling one in all the great best-sellers.

V.S. Pritchett

Biography and Autobiography

A well-written life is almost as rare as a well-spent one.
Thomas Carlyle

♦

Every great man nowadays has his disciples, and it is always Judas who writes the biography.

Oscar Wilde

♦

I have not much interest in anyone's personal history after the tenth year, not even my own. Whatever one was going to be was all prepared before that.

Katherine Anne Porter

Biography is to give a man some kind of shape after his death.

Virginia Woolf

◆

Biographies are but the clothes and buttons of the man—the biography of the man himself cannot be written.

Mark Twain

◆

Just as there is nothing between the admirable omelette and the intolerable, so with autobiography.

Hilaire Belloc

◆

Autobiography is an obituary in serial form with the last installment missing.

Quentin Crisp

◆

Autobiography is an unrivalled vehicle for telling the truth about other people.

Philip Guedalla

Only when one has lost all curiosity about the future has one reached the age to write an autobiography.

Evelyn Waugh

♦

A poet's autobiography is his poetry. Anything else can only be a footnote.

Yevgeny Yevtushenko

♦

Just how difficult it is to write biography can be reckoned by anybody who sits down and considers just how many people know the real truth about his or her love affairs.

Rebecca West

Henry Miller

(1891–1980)

I've led a good rich sexual life and I don't see why it should be left out.

Books

A book ought to be an icepick to break up the frozen sea within us.

Franz Kafka

♦

Books are...funny little portable pieces of thought.

Susan Sontag

♦

I have always come to life after coming to books.

Jorge Luis Borges

♦

A successful book cannot afford to be more than ten percent new.

Marshall McLuhan

♦

The possession of a book becomes a substitute for reading it.

Anthony Burgess

No furniture is so charming as books.

Sydney Smith

♦

Some books are undeservedly forgotten; none are undeservedly remembered.

W.H. Auden

♦

Books should to one of these four ends conduce,
For wisdom, piety, delight or use.

John Denham

♦

The reason why so few good books are written is that so few people who can write know anything.

Walter Bagehot

♦

There are books of which the backs and covers are by far the best parts.

Charles Dickens

♦

Books without knowledge of life are useless.

Ben Jonson

Books, nowadays, are printed by people who do not understand them, sold by people who do not understand them, read and reviewed by people who do not understand them, and even written by people who do not understand them.

G.C. Lichtenberg

◆

Until one has some kind of professional relationship with books, one does not discover how bad the majority of them are.

George Orwell

◆

A book is a mirror: if an ass peers into it, you can't expect an apostle to look out.

G.C. Lichtenberg

◆

Never read any book that is not a year old.

Ralph Waldo Emerson

◆

Never lend books, for no one ever returns them; the only books I have in my library are books that other folk have lent me.

Anatole France

Hard-covered books break up friendships. You loan a hard-covered book to a friend and when he doesn't return it you get mad at him. It makes you mean and petty. But twenty-five cent books are different.

John Steinbeck

♦

The oldest books are still only just out to those who have not read them.

Samuel Butler

♦

A good book is the precious life-blood of a master spirit, embalmed and treasured up on purpose to a life beyond life.

John Milton

♦

Books think for me.

Charles Lamb

♦

The road to ignorance is paved with good editions.

George Bernard Shaw

♦

A man's library is a sort of harem, and tender readers have a great prudency in showing their books to a stranger.

Ralph Waldo Emerson

A bad book is as much a labor to write as a good one; it comes as sincerely from the author's soul.

Aldous Huxley

♦

A great book should leave you with many experiences, and slightly exhausted at the end.

William Styron

♦

Americans like fat books and thin women.

Russell Baker

Censorship

The dirtiest book of all is the expurgated book.

Walt Whitman

♦

The books that the world calls immoral are the books that show the world its own shame.

Oscar Wilde

♦

Give me the liberty to know, to utter, and to argue freely according to conscience, above all liberties.

John Milton

♦

No member of society has a right to teach any doctrine contrary to what society holds to be true.

Samuel Johnson

Persons who undertake to pry into, or cleanse out all the filth of a common sewer, either cannot have very nice noses, or will soon lose them.

William Hazlitt

♦

Knowledge cannot defile, nor consequently the books, if the will and conscience be not defiled.

John Milton

♦

Those whom books will hurt will not be proof against events. If some books are deemed more baneful and their sale forbid, how, then, with deadlier facts, not dreams of doting men? Events, not books, should be forbid.

Herman Melville

♦

Assassination is the extreme form of censorship.

George Bernard Shaw

Characters

You can never know enough about your characters.
W. Somerset Maugham

♦

If a writer is true to his characters they will give him his plot. Observations must play second fiddle to integrity.
Phyllis Bottome

♦

I don't feel sympathetic toward some characters, unsympathetic toward others. I don't love some characters, feel contempt for others. They have attitudes; I don't.
Don DeLillo

♦

Begin with an individual and you find that you have created a type; begin with a type and you find that you have created—nothing.
F. Scott Fitzgerald

Of course I base my characters partly on the people I know—one can't escape it—but fictional characters are over-simplified; they're much less complex than the people one knows.

Aldous Huxley

♦

I sometimes lose interest in the characters and get much more interested in the trees and animals.

Toni Morrison

♦

When I used to teach creative writing, I would tell the students to make their characters want something right away—even if it's only a glass of water. Characters paralyzed by the meaninglessness of modern life still have to drink water from time to time.

Kurt Vonnegut

♦

Each writer is born with a repertory company in his head and...as you get older, you become more skillful in casting them.

Gore Vidal

Daphne Du Maurier

(1907–1989)

It is true that I immersed myself in the characters, especially in the narrator, but then this has happened throughout my writing career. I lose myself in the plot as it unfolds.

I don't have a very clear idea of who the characters are until they start talking.

Joan Didion

♦

You can't blame a writer for what the characters say.

Truman Capote

♦

As much as I can give of myself I give of myself. There's no reason why not. And when I have to hide something, I let the character speak.

Isaac Bashevis Singer

♦

Many of the characters are fools and they are always playing tricks on me and treating me badly.

Jorge Luis Borges

♦

That trite little whimsy about characters getting out of hand; it is as old as the quills. My characters are galley slaves.

Vladimir Nabokov

♦

My characters exasperate me.

Anita Brookner

The legend that characters run away from their authors—taking up drugs, having sex operations, and becoming president—implies that the writer is a fool with no knowledge or mastery of his craft. The idea of authors running around helplessly behind their cretinous inventions is contemptible.

John Cheever

♦

The characters have their own lives and their own logic, and you have to act accordingly.

Isaac Bashevis Singer

♦

Naming your characters Aristotle and Plato is not going to make their relationship interesting unless you make it so on the page.

Annie Dillard

♦

To pass judgment on people or characters in a book is to make silhouettes of them.

Cesare Pavese

♦

Fuck structure and grab your characters by the time balls.

Jack Kerouac

Colleagues

The language of Aristophanes reeks of his miserable quackery: it is made up of the lowest and most miserable puns; he doesn't even please the people, and to men of judgment and honor he is intolerable; his arrogance is insufferable, and all honest men detest his malice.

Plutarch

◆

The graces once made up their mind
A shrine inviolate to find:
And thus they found, and that with ease,
The soul of Aristophanes.

Plato

◆

Cicero's style bores me. When I have spent an hour reading him...and try to recollect what I have extracted, I usually find it nothing but wind.

Montaigne

Seneca I've never been able to take seriously. I've always thought that he really belonged in the old-time Hearst Sunday supplement, or in one of the lower order of fantasy and science fiction magazines.

Kenneth Rexroth

♦

Dante makes me sick.

Lope de Vega

♦

I'll bet Shakespeare compromised himself a lot; anybody who's in the entertainment industry does to some extent.

Christopher Isherwood

♦

Shakespeare never has six lines together without a fault.

Samuel Johnson

♦

Shakespeare was a dramatist of note;
He lived by writing things to quote.

H.C. Bunner

♦

If Bacon wrote Shakespeare, who wrote Bacon?

George Lyman Kittredge

I don't know if Bacon wrote the works of Shakespeare, but if he did not, he missed the opportunity of his life.

James M. Barrie

♦

If the public likes you, you're good. Shakespeare was a common, down-to-earth writer in his day.

Mickey Spillane

♦

Macbeth is a tale told by a genius, full of soundness and fury, signifying many things.

James Thurber

♦

To this day I cannot read *King Lear,* having had the advantage of studying it accurately in school.

Alfred North Whitehead

♦

Poets like Shakespeare knew more about psychiatry than any $25-an-hour man.

Robert Frost

♦

To know the force of human genius we should read Shakespeare; to see the insignificance of human learning we may study his commentators.

William Hazlitt

To read Dryden, Pope, etc., you need only count syllables; but to read Donne you must measure *time,* and discover the time of each word by the sense of passion.

Samuel Taylor Coleridge

♦

I have not wasted my life trifling with literary fools in taverns as Jonson did when he should have been shaking England with the thunder of his spirit.

George Bernard Shaw

♦

George Wither was taken prisoner, and was in danger of his life, having written severely against the king. Sir John Denham went to the king, and desired his majesty not to hang him, for that whilst G.W. lived he should not be the worst poet in England.

John Aubrey

♦

His imagination resembles the wings of an ostrich.

Thomas Babington Macaulay on John Dryden

Steele might become a reasonably good writer if he would pay a little more attention to grammar, learn something about the propriety and disposition of words and, incidentally, get some information on the subject he intends to handle.

Jonathan Swift on Richard Steele

♦

No author ever spared a brother;
Wits and gamecocks to one another.

John Gay

♦

Pope came off clean with Homer; but they say
Broome went before, and kindly swept the way.

J. Henley

♦

His more ambitious works may be defined as careless thinking carefully versified.

James Russell Lowell on Alexander Pope

♦

You have but two subjects, yourself and me. I am sick of both.

Samuel Johnson to James Boswell

Schiller's blank verse is bad. He moves in it as a fly in a glue bottle. His thoughts have their connection and variety, it is true, but there is no sufficiently corresponding movement in the verse.

Samuel Taylor Coleridge

♦

In his youth, Wordsworth sympathized with the French Revolution, went to France, wrote good poetry and had a natural daughter. At this period, he was a "bad" man. Then he became "good," abandoned his daughter, adopted correct principles and wrote bad poetry.

Bertrand Russell

♦

Carlyle is the same old sausage, fizzing and sputtering in his own grease.

Henry James

♦

From the poetry of Lord Byron they drew a system of ethics compounded of misanthropy and voluptuousness—a system in which the two greatest commandments were to hate your neighbor and to love your neighbor's wife.

Thomas Babington Macaulay

That dirty little blackguard.

Lord Byron on John Keats

♦

I became interested in syphilis when I worked for a time at a mental hospital full of GPI cases. I discovered there was a correlation between the spirochete and mad talent. The tubercule also produces a lyrical drive. Keats had both.

Anthony Burgess

♦

Such writing is mental masturbation—he is always fr-gg-g his Imagination. I don't mean he is indecent, but viciously soliciting his own ideas into a state, which is neither poetry nor anything else but a Bedlam vision produced by raw pork and opium.

Lord Byron on John Keats

♦

Shelley I saw once. His voice was the most obnoxious squeak I ever was tormented with.

Charles Lamb

♦

He was a liar and a cheat; he paid no regard to truth, nor to any kind of moral obligation.

Robert Southey on Percy Bysshe Shelley

Tennyson is a beautiful half of a poet.

Ralph Waldo Emerson

◆

Mr. Whitman's muse is at once indecent and ugly, lascivious and gawky, lubricious and coarse.

Lafcadio Hearn

◆

An agile but unintelligent and abnormal German, possessed of the mania of grandeur.

Leo Tolstoy on Friedrich Wilhelm Nietzsche

◆

Rilke was the greatest Lesbian poet since Sappho.

W.H. Auden

◆

I am seldom interested in what he is saying, but only in the way he says it.

T.S. Eliot on Ezra Pound

◆

T.S. Eliot owes almost everything to Pound.

Truman Capote

Both T.S. Eliot and I like to play, but I like to play euchre, while he likes to play Eucharist.

Robert Frost

♦

The cruelest thing that has happened to Lincoln since he was shot by Booth was to fall into the hands of Carl Sandburg.

Edmund Wilson

♦

The high-water mark, so to speak, of Socialist literature is W.H. Auden, a sort of gutless Kipling.

George Orwell

♦

I am fairly unrepentant about her poetry. I really think that three quarters of it is gibberish. However, I must crush down these thoughts otherwise the dove of peace will shit on me.

Noel Coward on Edith Sitwell

♦

So you've been reviewing Edith Sitwell's latest piece of virgin dung, have you? Isn't she a poisonous thing of a woman, lying, concealing, flipping, plagiarizing, misquoting and being as clever a crooked literary publicist as ever?

Dylan Thomas

If it were thought that anything I wrote was influenced by Robert Frost, I would take that particular work of mine, shred it, and flush it down the toilet, hoping not to clog the pipes. A more sententious, holding-forth old bore who expected every hero-worshiping adenoidal little twerp of a student-poet to hang on his every word I never saw.

James Dickey

♦

He was a very mean man. Everybody that ever knew him at all will tell you that.

Truman Capote on Robert Frost

♦

Dylan Thomas once told me that poets only know two kinds of birds by sight; one is a robin and the other a seagull, he said, and the rest of them he had to look up.

Lawrence Durrell

♦

He's the only poet that I've ever known in the universe who simply did not drink.

John Berryman on Randall Jarrell

I find it distressing to remember that this writer of genius regularly compared herself with writers who were in no way her peers and was upset by their success and longed for a certain kind of commercial success which was so much less than what she deserved.

Susan Sontag on Sylvia Plath

◆

Yevtushenko has...an ego that can crack crystal at a distance of twenty feet.

John Cheever

◆

Poets, like whores, are only hated by each other.

William Wycherley

◆

My heroes are poets. I have rejoiced in the privilege, unearned, of spending evenings with Eliot, days and weeks with Auden, occasions with Cocteau, hours with Dylan Thomas, Robert Graves, Robert Lowell, Joseph Brodsky, Eugenio Montale, Ingeborg Bachmann. I venerate them all.

Robert Craft

He has occasional flashes of silence that make his conversation perfectly delightful.

Sydney Smith on Thomas Babington Macaulay

♦

A glittering humbug.

Thomas Carlyle on Victor Hugo

♦

One must have a heart of stone to read the death of Little Nell by Dickens without laughing.

Oscar Wilde

♦

Dickens was the incarnation of cockneydom, a caricaturist who aped the moralist; he should have kept to short stories. If his novels are read at all in the future people will wonder what we saw in him.

George Meredith

♦

The four greatest novelists the world has ever known—Balzac, Dickens, Tolstoy and Dostoevski—wrote their respective languages very badly.

W. Somerset Maugham

His style is chaos, illuminated by flashes of lightning. As a writer he has mastered everything except language; as a novelist he can do everything except tell a story; as an artist he is everything, except articulate.

Oscar Wilde on George Meredith

♦

Poor Matt, he's gone to Heaven, no doubt—but he won't like God.

Robert Louis Stevenson on Matthew Arnold

♦

His work is evil, and he is one of those unhappy beings of whom one can say that it would have been better had he never been born.

Anatole France on Émile Zola

♦

Henry James had a mind so fine that no idea could violate it.
T.S. Eliot

♦

Henry James was one of the nicest old ladies I ever met.
William Faulkner

♦

Mr. Henry James writes fiction as if it were a painful duty.
Oscar Wilde

I am reading Henry James...and feel myself as one entombed in a block of smooth amber.

Virginia Woolf

◆

Poor Henry, he's spending eternity wandering round and round a stately park and the fence is just too high for him to peep over and they're having tea just too far away for him to hear what the Countess is saying.

W. Somerset Maugham

◆

Henry James would have been vastly improved as a novelist by a few whiffs from the Chicago stockyards.

H.L. Mencken

◆

I have the reputation of having read all of Henry James. Which would argue a misspent youth *and* middle age.

James Thurber

◆

He festooned the dung heap on which he had placed himself with sonnets as people grow honeysuckle around outdoor privies.

Quentin Crisp on Oscar Wilde

What a tiresome, affected sod.

Noel Coward on Oscar Wilde

♦

You have to be over thirty to enjoy Proust.

Gore Vidal

♦

I was reading Proust for the first time. Very poor stuff. I think he was mentally defective.

Evelyn Waugh

♦

Mr. Conrad has paid us a pretty compliment by learning to write the English language correctly, and the journalists are so pleased that they have assigned him a place in our literature.

George Moore

♦

He wasn't exactly hostile to facts, but he was apathetic about them.

Wolcott Gibbs on Alexander Woollcott

He became mellow before he became ripe.
> *Alexander Woollcott* on Christopher Morley

♦

Bernard Shaw has no enemies but is intensely disliked by his friends.

> *Oscar Wilde*

♦

It is his life work to announce the obvious in terms of the scandalous.
> *H.L. Mencken* on George Bernard Shaw

♦

Mr. Shaw is (I suspect) the only man on earth who has never written any poetry.

> *G.K. Chesterton*

♦

The more I think you over the more it comes home to me what an unmitigated Middle Victorian ass you are!
> *H.G. Wells* to George Bernard Shaw

♦

Inconceivable as it may seem, I found Shaw an awful bore.
> *H.G. Wells*

Nobody can read Freud without realizing that he was the scientific equivalent of another nuisance, George Bernard Shaw.

Robert Maynard Hutchins

♦

He writes his plays for the ages—the ages between five and twelve.

George Jean Nathan on George Bernard Shaw

♦

H.L. Mencken suffers from the hallucination that he is H.L. Mencken—there is no cure for a disease of that magnitude.

Maxwell Bodenheim

♦

Kafka was possessed by. . .inhibitions. They impeded him in everything he did—in sex as well as in writing. He craved love and fled from it. He wrote a sentence and immediately crossed it out.

Isaac Bashevis Singer

♦

I like him, but one Kafka in a century is enough.

Isaac Bashevis Singer

The greatest female writer in America now—but just wait until next year.

Carson McCullers on Katherine Anne Porter

♦

Hammett took murder out of the parlor and put it in the alley where it belongs.

Raymond Chandler

♦

His style has the desperate jauntiness of an orchestra fiddling away for dear life on a sinking ship.

Edmund Wilson on Evelyn Waugh

♦

You should approach Joyce's *Ulysses* as the illiterate Baptist preacher approaches the Old Testament: with faith.

William Faulkner

♦

James Joyce—an essentially private man who wished his total indifference to public notice to be universally recognized.

Tom Stoppard

My God, what a clumsy olla putrida James Joyce is! Nothing but old fags and cabbage stumps of quotations from the Bible and the rest, stewed in the juice of deliberate, journalistic dirty-mindedness.

D.H. Lawrence

♦

English literature's performing flea.

Sean O'Casey on P.G. Wodehouse

♦

Your novel has every fault the English novel can have...a rotten work of genius.

Ford Madox Ford to D.H. Lawrence

♦

Freud Madox Fraud.

Osbert Sitwell

♦

I loathe you. You revolt me stewing in your consumption...the Italians were quite right to have nothing to do with you. You are a loathsome reptile—I hope you will die.

D.H. Lawrence to Katherine Mansfield

Dorothy Parker

(1893–1967)

I was following in the exquisite footsteps of Miss Edna
St. Vincent Millay, unhappily in my own horrible
sneakers.

Rebecca West: I've never been able to do just one draft. Do you know anyone who can?

Interviewer: I think D.H. Lawrence did.

Rebecca West: You could often tell.

◆

He couldn't write for toffee, bless his heart.

Rebecca West on W. Somerset Maugham

◆

Sherwood Anderson never tried to please anybody—he considered it everybody's duty to please him.

Ben Hecht

◆

Gertrude Stein's prose is a cold, black suet-pudding. We can represent it as a cold suet-roll of fabulously reptilian length. Cut it at any point, it is...the same heavy, sticky, opaque mass all through, and all along.

Percy Wyndham Lewis

◆

Miss Stein was a past master at making nothing happen very slowly.

Clifton Fadiman

Hemingway? What did he do that made him so big? He wrote some good stuff, but what was so *big* about it? He never sold that many.

Mickey Spillane

♦

Hemingway's remarks are not literature.

Gertrude Stein

♦

I read him for the first time in the early forties, something about bells, balls and bulls, and loathed it.

Vladimir Nabokov on Ernest Hemingway

♦

He was an incredibly vain man.

John Steinbeck on Ernest Hemingway

♦

When his cock wouldn't stand up, he blew his head off. He sold himself a line of bullshit and bought it.

Germaine Greer on Ernest Hemingway

♦

He was the critics' darling because he never changed style, theme nor story. He made no experiments in thinking nor emotion.

John Steinbeck on Ernest Hemingway

Hemingway was a necromancer who adopted every superior Balzacian trick in the book, each technical device that Flaubert and Tolstoy and Dickens had found useful, so that quite often his work seemed better than it really was.

James Michener

♦

I detest him, but I was certainly under his spell when I was very young, as we all were. I thought his prose was perfect—until I read Stephen Crane and realized where he got it from.

Gore Vidal on Ernest Hemingway

♦

Hemingway had a remarkable interest in and understanding of homosexuality, for a man who wasn't a homosexual.

Tennessee Williams

♦

There was a mean man.

Truman Capote on Ernest Hemingway

♦

Thomas Wolfe has always seemed to me the most overrated, long-winded and boring of reputable American novelists.

Edith Oliver

If it must be Thomas, let it be Mann, and if it must be Wolfe let it be Nero, but never let it be Thomas Wolfe.

Peter De Vries

♦

Beckett writes short but exquisite things.

Pablo Neruda

♦

He writes by sanded fingertips.

Lillian Hellman on Tennessee Williams

♦

Odets, where is thy sting?

George S. Kaufman

♦

The only man who wrote a great deal in our time was John O'Hara, because he went on the wagon and had nothing else to do.

Irwin Shaw

♦

Hard to lay down but easy not to pick up.

Malcolm Cowley on John O'Hara's novels

You know the beginning of *Gatsby*, the little frontispiece? They say Fitzgerald made that up. I always thought that was such a great thing to do—make up a quote and pretend it really inspired you.

Nora Ephron

◆

Faulkner said more asinine things than any other major American writer. I can't remember a single interesting remark Faulkner ever made.

Norman Mailer

◆

Faulkner had a mean small Southern streak in him, and most of his pronunciamentos reflect that meanness. He's a great writer, but he's not all that interesting in most of his passing remarks.

Norman Mailer

◆

I knew Faulkner very well. He was a great friend of mine. Well, as much as you could be a friend of his, unless you were a fourteen-year-old nymphet.

Truman Capote

◆

Could Faulkner find a publisher now?

Annie Dillard

Capote should be heard, not read.

Gore Vidal

♦

Like Toulouse-Lautrec, he will come to represent his period, and he will be treasured for the masterly way he epitomized it.

James Michener on Truman Capote

♦

Truman is canny as hell, but he's not the brightest guy in the world.

Norman Mailer

♦

He thinks he's Bunny Mellon.

Gore Vidal on Truman Capote

♦

A Republican housewife from Kansas with all the prejudices.

Gore Vidal on Truman Capote

♦

He was a full-fledged master of the language before he was old enough to vote.

William Styron on Truman Capote

Truman Capote has made lying an art. A *minor* art.

Gore Vidal

◆

I think you judge Truman a bit too charitably when you call him a child: he is more like a sweetly vicious old lady.

Tennessee Williams

◆

We European innocents think of Truman Capote mainly as a writer. I know he is seen otherwise in America.

John Fowles

◆

He'd be all right if he took his finger out of his mouth.

Harold Robbins on Truman Capote

◆

He's a second-rate Stephen Birmingham. And Steven Birmingham is third-rate.

Truman Capote on Louis Auchincloss

◆

I'm told, on very good authority, that he hasn't stopped writing at all. That he's written at least five or six short novels and that all of them have been turned down by *The New Yorker.* And that all of them are very strange and about Zen Buddhism.

Truman Capote on J.D. Salinger

Norman Mailer thinks William Burroughs is a genius, which I think is ludicrous beyond words. I don't think William Burroughs has an ounce of talent.

Truman Capote

♦

That's not writing, that's typing.

Truman Capote on Jack Kerouac

♦

He had one of the more wicked minds ever going.

Truman Capote on Mark Twain

♦

She looks like a truck driver in drag.

Truman Capote on Jacqueline Susann

♦

Philip Roth is a marvelous writer but I'd hate to shake hands with him.

Jacqueline Susann after reading *Portnoy's Complaint*

♦

I'm glad there are people like Burroughs to take the dope and all so *I* don't have to do it.

John Barth

Nabokov's a real sport.

John Barth

♦

Nabokov graces his own novels as a figure—a figure at once majestic and ironic, the way Alfred Hitchcock appears in his own films.

Annie Dillard

♦

She writes like a middle-aged French *roué*. She writes like Carl Jung dreaming he is Candide.

John Barth on Susan Sontag

♦

He is a bad novelist and a fool. The combination usually makes for great popularity in the U.S.

Gore Vidal on Alexander Solzhenitsyn

♦

Borges is the only living successor to Franz Kafka.

Nadine Gordimer

♦

There is no living writer of whom I am simply in awe, except Günter Grass.

John Irving

♦

I haven't read many of my contemporaries. They haven't read me either, and so we are even.

John Barth

Competition

I don't feel in competition with other writers. Because I don't write about the same things as any other writer that I know of does.

Truman Capote

♦

Each writer is a separate entity. The mistake people like Mailer make is that writing is for him a track race.

William Styron

♦

I think about Tolstoy, Flaubert and Dickens, and I'm jealous of what those authors accomplished. Because I am jealous, I am a writer now. I remain jealous and this gives me a guide to what I might accomplish.

James Michener

I started out very quiet and I beat Mr. Turgenev. Then I trained hard and I beat Mr. de Maupassant. I've fought two draws with Mr. Stendhal, and I think I had an edge in the last one. But nobody's going to get me in any ring with Mr. Tolstoy unless I'm crazy or I keep getting better.

Ernest Hemingway

◆

I can write better than anyone who can write faster, and I can write faster than anyone who can write better.

A.J. Liebling

◆

Writing…is practically the only activity a person can do that is not competitive.

Paul Theroux

Critics
and
Criticism

*C*ritic, n. A person who boasts himself hard to please because nobody tries to please him.

Ambrose Bierce

♦

The first man who objected to the general nakedness and advised his fellows to put on clothes, was the first critic.

Edwin L. Godkin

♦

A critic is a man who expects miracles.

James Gibbons Huneker

♦

A critic is a gong at a railroad crossing clanging loudly and vainly as the train goes by.

Christopher Morley

Drooling, driveling, doleful, depressing, dropsical drips.
Sir Thomas Beecham

♦

These curious sucker fish who live with joyous vicarious-
ness on other men's work and discipline with dreary words
the thing which feeds them.

John Steinbeck

♦

A critic is a haunter of unquiet graves. He tries to evoke the
presence of a living art, but usually succeeds only in disturb-
ing the peace of the dead.

M.J.C. Hodgart

♦

Critics! Appalled I ventured on the name.
Those cutthroat bandits in the paths of fame.

Robert Burns

♦

A critic is a man created to praise greater men than himself,
but he is never able to find them.

Richard Le Gallienne

All the little congruences and arabesques you prepared with such delicate anticipatory pleasure are gobbled up as if by pigs at a pastry cart.

John Updike

♦

A critic is a necessary evil, and criticism is an evil necessity.

Carolyn Wells

♦

Reviewers...actually newspaper persons who chat about books in the press...have been with us from the beginning and they will be with us at the end. They are interested in writers, not writing. In good morals, not good art. When they like something of mine, I grow suspicious and wonder.

Gore Vidal

♦

The new race of academic reviewers may be cleverer, more conscientious, fairer than those who went before and they may take their job more seriously, but they are a complete disaster from everyone's point of view—publisher, book buyer, writer—because practically no one reads them. It is not just that they assume a higher dedication and a higher level of seriousness than exists among most intelligent, educated novel readers. They are quite simply too dull.

Auberon Waugh

Reviewers are not born but made, and they are made by editors.

Anthony Burgess

♦

A book reviewer is usually a barker before the door of a publisher's circus.

Austin O'Malley

♦

Reviewers are usually people who would have been poets, historians, biographers, etc., if they could; they have tried their talents at one or at the other, and have failed; therefore they turn critics.

Samuel Taylor Coleridge

♦

A dramatic critic is a man who leaves no turn unstoned.

George Bernard Shaw

♦

Has anybody ever seen a drama critic in the daytime? Of course not. They come out after dark, up to no good.

P.G. Wodehouse

There is not a single dramatic critic in London who would deliberately set himself to misrepresent the work of any dramatist—unless, of course, he personally disliked the dramatist.

Oscar Wilde

♦

A true critic hath one quality in common with a harlot, never to change his title or his nature.

Jonathan Swift

♦

The trade of critic, in literature, music, and the drama, is the most degraded of all trades.

Mark Twain

♦

Many a critic seems more like a committee framing resolutions than a man writing down what he thinks.

Frank Moore Colby

♦

The good critic is he who narrates the adventures of his soul among masterpieces.

Anatole France

The test of a good critic is whether he knows when and how
to believe on insufficient evidence.

Samuel Butler

♦

The only critics worth reading are the critics who practice,
and practice well, the art of which they write.

T.S. Eliot

♦

A good critic is the sorcerer that makes some hidden spring
gush forth unexpectedly under our feet.

François Mauriac

♦

Critics are probably more prone to clichés than fiction writers who pluck things out of the air.

Penelope Gillatt

♦

As soon
Seek roses in December—ice in June;
Hope constancy in wind, or corn in chaff;
Believe a woman or an epitaph,
Or any other thing that's false, before
You trust in critics.

Lord Byron

A man must serve his time at every trade save censure—
critics all are ready made.

Lord Byron

♦

An artist is born kneeling; he fights to stand. A critic, by
nature of the judgment seat, is born sitting.

Hortense Calisher

♦

A good writer is not, *per se,* a good book critic. No more than
a good drunk is automatically a good bartender.

Jim Bishop

♦

Those who write ill, and they who ne'er durst write,
Turn critics out of mere revenge and spite.

John Dryden

♦

Nature fits all her children with something to do,
He who would write and can't write, can surely review.

James Russell Lowell

Every good poet includes a critic, but the reverse will not hold.

William Shenstone

♦

To literary critics a book is assumed to be guilty until it proves itself innocent.

Nelson Algren

♦

One battle doesn't make a campaign, but critics treat one book, good or bad, like a whole war.

Ernest Hemingway

♦

I'll give you fifty dollars if you produce a writer who can honestly say he was ever helped by the prissy carpings and condescensions of reviewers.

Truman Capote

♦

I have been aided by some censorious but able reviewers who were willing to take pains in order to inflict them.

Frank Moore Colby

♦

The critic should describe, and not prescribe.

Eugène Ionesco

W. Somerset Maugham

(1874–1965)

One of the amusements of being old is that I have no illusions about my literary position. . . . I no longer mind what people think.

Critics of literature have the same essential function as teachers of literature: this is not to direct the judgment of the audience, but to assist the audience in those disciplines of reading on which any meaningful judgment must rest.

Mark Schorer

♦

An important job of the critic is to savage what is mediocre or meretricious.

Susan Sontag

♦

Critics sometimes appear to be addressing themselves to works other than those I remember writing.

Joyce Carol Oates

♦

There is probably no hell for authors in the next world—they suffer so much from critics and publishers in this one.

C.N. Bovee

♦

I can imagine nothing more distressing to a critic than to have a writer see accurately into his own work.

Norman Mailer

The only really difficult thing about a poem is the critic's explanation of it.

Frank Moore Colby

♦

When critics disagree, the artist is in accord with himself.

Oscar Wilde

♦

Time is the only critic without ambition.

John Steinbeck

♦

Mediocrity is more dangerous in a critic than in a writer.

Eugène Ionesco

♦

Show me a critic without prejudices, and I'll show you an arrested cretin.

George Jean Nathan

♦

For critics I care the five hundred thousandth part of the tythe of a half-farthing.

Charles Lamb

The lot of critics is to be remembered by what they failed to understand.

George Moore

♦

There's an almost unavoidable feeling of smugness, of self-satisfaction, of teacher's pettishness, that sinks into a critic's bones.

Irwin Shaw

♦

The best thing you can do about critics is never say a word. In the end you have the last say, and they know it.

Tennessee Williams

♦

Asking a working writer what he thinks about critics is like asking a lamppost what it feels about dogs.

John Osborne

♦

Criticism is a study by which men grow important and formidable at very small expense.

Samuel Johnson

Criticism is the art wherewith a critic tries to guess himself into a share of the artist's fame.

George Jean Nathan

♦

I am bound by my own definition of criticism: a disinterested endeavor to learn and propagate the best that is known and thought in the world.

Matthew Arnold

♦

The avocation of assessing the failures of better men can be turned into a comfortable livelihood, providing you back it up with a Ph.D.

Nelson Algren

♦

Writing criticism is to writing fiction and poetry as hugging the shore is to sailing the open sea.

John Updike

♦

A bad review by a man I admire hurts terribly.

Anthony Burgess

Books should be tried by a judge and jury as though they were crimes.

Samuel Butler

♦

A great deal of contemporary criticism reads to me like a man saying: "Of course I do not like green cheese; I am very fond of brown sherry."

G.K. Chesterton

♦

The main use in criticism is in showing what manner of man the critic is.

Frank Moore Colby

♦

I don't read my reviews, I measure them.

Joseph Conrad

♦

I love criticism just so long as it's unqualified praise.
Noel Coward

♦

I never read unpleasant things about myself.
Truman Capote

The artists who want to be writers, read the reviews; the artists who want to write, don't.

William Faulkner

♦

I read very few critics. Friendly but ignorant reviews of my books tell me nothing. Hostile reviews can, for a brief time, irritate me. Favorable reviews by authors I treasure make me happy for a while. But if they are people who mean nothing to me, they depress me.

Graham Greene

♦

A unanimous chorus of approval is not an assurance of survival; authors who please everyone at once are quickly exhausted.

André Gide

♦

When a man publishes a book, there are so many stupid things said that he declares he'll never do it again. The praise is almost always worse than the criticism.

Sherwood Anderson

I don't see how you can write anything of value if you don't offend someone.

Marvin Harris

♦

Reading reviews of your own book is. . .a no-win game. If the review is flattering, one tends to feel vain and uneasy. If it is bad, one tends to feel exposed, found out. Neither feeling does you any good.

Walker Percy

♦

It is advantageous to an author that his book should be attacked as well as praised. Fame is a shuttlecock. If it be struck at only one end of the room, it will soon fall to the ground. To keep it up, it must be struck at both ends.

Samuel Johnson

♦

You do not get a man's most effective criticism until you provoke him. Severe truth is expressed with some bitterness.

Henry David Thoreau

♦

The man who is asked by an author what he thinks of his work is not obliged to speak the truth.

Samuel Johnson

People ask you for criticism but they only want praise.
W. Somerset Maugham

◆

You may scold a carpenter who has made you a bad table, though you cannot make a table. It is not your trade to make tables.
Samuel Johnson

◆

When I dislike what I see on the stage, I can be vastly amusing, but when I write about something I like, I am appallingly dull.
Max Beerbohm

◆

Your manuscript is both good and original; but the part that is good is not original, and the part that is original is not good.
Samuel Johnson

◆

When I have to praise a writer, I usually do it by attacking his enemies.
H.L. Mencken

Confronted by an absolutely infuriating review it is sometimes helpful for the victim to do a little personal research on the critic. Is there any truth to the rumor that he had no formal education beyond the age of eleven? In any event, is he able to construct a simple English sentence? Do his participles dangle? When moved to lyricism does he write "I had a fun time"? Was he ever arrested for burglary? I don't know that you will prove anything this way, but it is perfectly harmless and quite soothing.

Jean Kerr

♦

One of the greatest creations of the human mind is the art of reviewing books without having to read them.

G.C. Lichtenberg

♦

I never read a book before reviewing it. It prejudices me so.

Sydney Smith

♦

Ideal dramatic criticism is unqualified appreciation.

Oscar Wilde

Honest criticism means nothing; what one wants is unrestrained passion, fire for fire.

Henry Miller

♦

I like criticism, but it must be my way.

Mark Twain

♦

I find criticism most instructive when an expert proves to me that my facts or my grammar are wrong.

Vladimir Nabokov

♦

You don't so much review a play as draw up a crushing brief against it.

Edmund Wilson

♦

Anyone can be accurate and even profound, but it is damned hard work to make criticism charming.

H.L. Mencken

♦

Criticism can be instructive in the sense that it gives readers, including the author of the book, some information about the critic's intelligence, or honesty, or both.

Vladimir Nabokov

'Tis hard to say if greater want of skill
Appear in writing or judging ill.

Alexander Pope

♦

Reviewing has one advantage over suicide: in suicide you take it out of yourself; in reviewing you take it out of other people.

George Bernard Shaw

♦

Everything is infinitely fine, and any opinion is somehow coarser than the texture of the real thing.

John Updike

♦

Why did all these giants descend on me and my little stories? I wasn't doing anything of national import. All I was trying to do was entertain the public and make a buck.

Mickey Spillane

♦

Of all the cants which are canted in this canting world—though the cant of hypocrites may be the worst—the cant of criticism is the most tormenting.

Laurence Sterne

I cannot greatly care what the critics say of my work; if it is good, it will come to the surface in a generation or two and float, and if not, it will sink, having in the meantime provided me with a living, the opportunities of leisure, and a craftsman's intimate satisfactions.

John Updike

♦

You can't go around saying you're a writer if no one will take you seriously.

William Kennedy

Drink

M any contemporary authors drink more than they write.

Maxim Gorky

♦

B oozing does not necessarily have to go hand in hand with being a writer, as seems to be the concept in America. I therefore solemnly declare to all young men trying to become writers that they do not actually have to become drunkards first.

James Jones

♦

I don't drink a lot. That's perhaps one of the reasons why my characters are always drinking and taking drugs, because I am not.

Robert Stone

Drinking makes you loquacious, as we all know, and if what you've got for company is a piece of paper, then you're going to talk to it. Just try to enunciate, and try to make sense.

Madison Smartt Bell

♦

I have never written a serious word in my life under the influence of alcohol.

William Styron

♦

I cannot write intoxicated in any way.

Robert Stone

♦

I usually need a can of beer to prime me.

Norman Mailer

♦

A man's prose style is very responsive—even a glass of sherry shows in a sentence.

John Cheever

♦

I never write when I'm drunk.

W.H. Auden

No one, ever, wrote anything as well even after one drink as he would have done without it.

Ring Lardner

♦

I've gone on the wagon, but my body doesn't believe it. It's waiting for that whiskey to get in there...to get me going. I never drink while I'm working, but after a few glasses, I get ideas that would never have occurred to me dead sober.

Irwin Shaw

♦

Faulkner was a big drinker, went on wild binges but he never wrote much while drunk. He and others drank to broaden their vision, their exaltation or despair, or to flee from the agony of the pure pain of creation.

William Styron

♦

When I have one martini, I feel bigger, wiser, taller. When I have a second, I feel superlative. When I have more, there's no holding me.

William Faulkner

Some American writers who have known each other for years have never met in the daytime or when both were sober.

James Thurber

◆

Before I start to write, I always treat myself to a nice dry martini. Just one, to give me the courage to get started. After that, I am on my own.

E.B. White

◆

After a few ounces, the old tunes wake up, the grandeur of jingling anguish, the lick and shimmer of language, the heartbreak at the core of things.... At a certain glow-level my brilliancies assured me I was an angel writing in Paradise.

Donald Newlove

◆

One of the disadvantages of wine is that it makes a man mistake words for thoughts.

Samuel Johnson

◆

I can't write without wine.

Tennessee Williams

Editors and Editing

My definition of a good editor is a man I think charming, who sends me large checks, praises my work, my physical beauty, and my sexual prowess, and who has a stranglehold on the publisher and the bank.

John Cheever

♦

Some writers like a good deal of help from their editors, others, like myself, reject it. Editors inhabit the publishing world, have lunch and cocktails together, and represent the opinions and attitudes of their class. Or its prejudices. Some writers want to imbibe these prejudices and feel them to be beneficial. The young writer is apt to feel helpless and dependent and opens his mouth like a young bird. The publishing industry feeds him a certain number of worms.

John Barth

An editor should tell the author his writing is better than
it is. Not a lot better, a little better.

T.S. Eliot

♦

Never buy an editor or publisher a lunch or a drink until
he has bought an article, story or book from you. This rule
is absolute and may be broken only at your peril.

John Creasey

♦

I usually have poor to absent relations with editors because
they have a habit of desiring changes and I resist changes.

William Gass

♦

No passion in the world is equal to the passion to alter someone else's draft.

H.G. Wells

♦

Every abridgement of a good book is a stupid abridgement.

Montaigne

Ego

Every author, however modest, keeps a most outrageous vanity chained like a madman in the padded cell of his breast.

Logan Pearsall Smith

♦

My problem is intense vanity and narcissism. I've always had such a good physique and such intense charm that it's difficult to be true to myself.

Lawrence Durrell

♦

I am an enormously talented man, after all it's no use pretending that I am not and I was bound to succeed.

Noel Coward

I've known all my life I could take a bunch of words and throw them up in the air and they would come down just right. I'm a semantic Paganini.

Truman Capote

♦

I'm the most translated writer in the world, behind Lenin, Tolstoy, Gorki and Jules Verne. And they're all dead.

Mickey Spillane

♦

No poet or novelist wishes he was the only one who ever lived, but most of them wish they were the only one alive, and quite a number fondly believe their wish has been granted.

W.H. Auden

♦

I am very foolish over my own book. I have a copy which I constantly read and find very illuminating. Swift confesses to something of the sort with his own compositions.

W.B. Yeats

♦

Writers become idiotic under flattery sooner than any other set of people in the world.

Frank Moore Colby

Writers are too self-centered to be lonely.

Richard Condon

♦

Every writer thinks he is capable of anything. Scratch a Faulkner or a Hemingway and you'll find a man who thinks he can run the world.

Norman Mailer

♦

Writing a novel, especially a long novel, is an immense act of ego. You're not only asking people to pursue your vision, you're also asking them to pay to do so—and to applaud.

William Gaddis

Fame

Fame is a vapor, popularity an accident; the only earthly certainty is oblivion.

Mark Twain

♦

Fame is a bee
It has a song—
It has a sting—
Ah, too, it has a wing.

Emily Dickinson

♦

I want it.

Tobi Sanders

♦

First you're unknown, then you write one book and you move up to obscurity.

Martin Myers

A writer is always admired most, not by those who have read him, but by those who have merely heard about him.

H.L. Mencken

♦

When audiences come to see us authors lecture, it is largely in the hope that we'll be funnier to look at than to read.

Sinclair Lewis

♦

It took me fifteen years to discover I had no talent for writing, but I couldn't give it up because by that time I was too famous.

Robert Benchley

♦

Lolita is famous, not I. I am an obscure, double obscure, novelist with an unpronounceable name.

Vladimir Nabokov

♦

Odd things happen to book writers when they become famous.

Ronald Sukenick

Early acclaim won't harm a writer if he has the strength, or the cynicism, not to believe in that acclaim.

Martin Amis

◆

In my district of Gascony, it is thought a joke to see me in print. The further from my home the knowledge of me travels, the higher I am valued.

Montaigne

◆

Little presses write to me for manuscripts and when I write back that I haven't any, they write to ask if they can print the letter saying I haven't any.

John Steinbeck

◆

If I could I would always work in silence and obscurity, and let my efforts be known by their results.

Emily Brontë

◆

Writers should be read—but neither seen nor heard.

Daphne du Maurier

◆

One should never be known by sight.

Henry Green

I like to be able to listen to conversations without people turning around to look at me over their shoulders. I want to be the man behind you in the fish shop.

Len Deighton

♦

It's a short walk from the hallelujah to the hoot.

Vladimir Nabokov

Fiction

Fiction is history without tables, graphs, dates, imports, edicts, evidence, laws; history without hiatus—intelligible, simple, smooth.

William Gass

♦

All fiction for me is a kind of magic and trickery—a confidence trick, trying to make people believe something is true that isn't.

Angus Wilson

♦

I am not interested in fiction. I want faithfulness.

Anaïs Nin

♦

Some things can only be said in fiction, but that doesn't mean they aren't true.

Aaron Latham

A wondrous dream, a fantasy incarnate, fiction completes us, mutilated beings burdened with the awful dichotomy of having only one life and the ability to desire a thousand.

Mario Vargas Llosa

◆

Fiction reveals truths that reality obscures.

Jessamyn West

◆

Truth may be stranger than fiction, but fiction is truer.

Frederic Raphael

◆

Why *shouldn't* truth be stranger than fiction? Fiction, after all, has to make sense.

Mark Twain

◆

The truth is, we've not really developed a fiction that can accommodate the full tumult, the zaniness and crazed quality of modern experience.

Saul Bellow

◆

The trouble with fiction is that it makes too much sense, whereas reality never makes sense.

Aldous Huxley

Ben Hecht

(1894–1964)

The sad thing about writing fiction is that unless one writes classics one writes in a closet. Nothing can disappear like a book.

All that non-fiction can do is answer questions. It's fiction's business to ask them.

Richard Hughes

◆

Stories ought to judge and interpret the world.

Cynthia Ozick

◆

The good end happily, the bad unhappily—that is what fiction means.

Oscar Wilde

◆

Fiction is nothing less than the subtlest instrument for self-examination and self-display that mankind has invented yet. Psychology and X-rays bring up some portentous shadows, and demographics and stroboscopic photography do some fine breakdowns, but for the full *parfum* and effluvia of being human, for feathery ambiguity and rank facticity, for the air and iron, fire and spit of our daily mortal adventure there is nothing like fiction: it makes sociology look priggish, history problematical, the film media two-dimensional, and the *National Enquirer* as silly as last week's cereal box.

John Updike

Genres

All the historical books which contain no lies are extremely tedious.

Anatole France

♦

What makes a good writer of history is a guy who is suspicious. Suspicion marks the real difference between the man who wants to write honest history and the one who'd rather write a good story.

Jim Bishop

♦

There's great scope in the historical novel, so long as it isn't by Mary Renault or Georgette Heyer.

Anthony Burgess

Historical fiction is not only a respectable literary form; it is a standing reminder of the fact that history is about human beings.

Helen M. Cam

♦

A historical romance is the only kind of book where chastity really counts.

Barbara Cartland

♦

Satire is always as sterile as it is shameful and is impotent as it is insolent.

Oscar Wilde

♦

Satire is what closes on Saturday night.

George S. Kaufman

♦

There exists an inverse correlation between the size of a ball and the quality of writing about the sport in which the ball is used. There are superb books about golf, very good books about baseball, not very many good books about football, few good books about basketball, and no good books on beachballs.

George Plimpton

The essay is a literary device for saying almost everything about almost anything.

Aldous Huxley

♦

The beginner who submits a detective novel longer than 80,000 words is courting rejection.

Howard Haycraft

♦

Love interest nearly always weakens a mystery because it introduces a type of suspense that is antagonistic to the detective's struggle to solve a problem.

Raymond Chandler

♦

The thriller is an extension of the fairy tale. It is melodrama so embellished as to create the illusion that the story being told, however unlikely, could be true.

Eric Ambler

♦

Frankly, I am not one of those college professors who coyly boasts of enjoying detective stories—they are too badly written for my taste and bore me to death.

Vladimir Nabokov

At least half the mystery novels published violate the law that the solution, once revealed, must seem to be inevitable.

Raymond Chandler

♦

The mystery story is really two stories in one: the story of what happened and the story of what appeared to happen.

Mary Roberts Rinehart

♦

There certainly does seem a possibility that the detective story will come to an end, simply because the public will have learnt all the tricks.

Dorothy Sayers

♦

Nobody reads a mystery to get to the middle. They read it to get to the end. If it's a letdown, they won't buy anymore. The first page sells that book. The last page sells your next book.

Mickey Spillane

♦

The detective himself should never turn out to be the culprit.

S.S. Van Dine

To accept a mediocre form and make something like literature out of it is in itself rather an accomplishment.

Raymond Chandler

♦

Fantasy is literature for teenagers.

Brian Aldiss

♦

A good science fiction story is a story with a human problem, and a human solution, which would not have happened without its science content.

Theodore Sturgeon

♦

I...don't particularly care for science fiction. I read some Jules Verne in my youth, but I'm not very interested in other planets. I like them where they are, in the sky.

W.H. Auden

Good Writing

Good writing is a kind of skating which carries off the performer where he would not go.

Ralph Waldo Emerson

♦

Good writing is supposed to evoke sensation in the reader—not the fact that it's raining, but the feel of being rained upon.

E.L. Doctorow

♦

Good writing is true writing. If a man is making a story up it will be true in proportion to the amount of knowledge of life that he has had and how conscientious he is; so that when he makes something up it is as it would truly be.

Ernest Hemingway

True ease in writing comes from art, not chance,
As those move easiest who have learned to dance.
'Tis not enough no harshness gives offence,
The sound must seem an echo to the sense.

Alexander Pope

♦

All good writing is *swimming under water* and holding your breath.

F. Scott Fitzgerald

♦

The secret of good writing is to say an old thing a new way or to say a new thing an old way.

Richard Harding Davis

♦

We like that a sentence should read as if its author, had he held a plough instead of a pen, could have drawn a furrow deep and straight to the end.

Henry David Thoreau

Good writing excites me, and makes life worth living.
                                        Harold Pinter

◆

Every fine story must leave in the mind of the sensitive reader an intangible residuum of pleasure, a cadence, a quality of voice that is exclusively the writer's own, individual, unique.

                                        Willa Cather

◆

People do not deserve good writing, they are so pleased with bad.

                                        Ralph Waldo Emerson

George Orwell

(1903–1950)

The great enemy of clear language is insincerity. When there is a gap between one's real and one's declared aims, one turns, as it were, instinctively to long words and exhausted idioms, like a cuttlefish squirting out ink.

Grammar

Grammar is the grave of letters.

Elbert Hubbard

♦

Any fool can make a rule and every fool will mind it.

Henry David Thoreau

♦

I don't know any but the simplest rules of English grammar, and I seldom consciously apply them. Nevertheless, I instinctively write correctly and, I like to think, in an interesting fashion. I know when something sounds right and when it doesn't, and I can tell the difference without hesitation, even when writing at breakneck speed. How do I do this? I haven't the faintest idea.

Isaac Asimov

Usage is the only test. I prefer a phrase that is easy and un-affected to a phrase that is grammatical.

W. Somerset Maugham

♦

Why care for grammar as long as we are good?

Artemus Ward

♦

You can be a little ungrammatical if you come from the right part of the country.

Robert Frost

♦

Grammar is a piano I play by ear. All I know about grammar is its power.

Joan Didion

♦

Word has somehow got around that the split infinitive is always wrong. That is a piece with the outworn notion that it is always wrong to strike a lady.

James Thurber

Hollywood

I went out there for a thousand a week, and I worked Monday, and I got fired Wednesday. The guy that hired me was out of town Tuesday.

Nelson Algren

♦

A dreary industrial town controlled by hoodlums of enormous wealth, the ethical sense of a pack of jackals, and taste so degraded that it befouled everything it touched.

S.J. Perelman

♦

I'm a Hollywood writer; so I put on a sports jacket and take off my brain.

Ben Hecht

Hollywood has the finest brains in the world out there. But they're up against all these vested interests, and vested interests are the very devil for the artist.

Frank O'Connor

♦

My principal feeling about Hollywood is suicide. If I could get out of bed and into the shower, I was all right. Since I never paid the bills, I'd reach for the phone and order the most elaborate breakfast I could think of, and then I'd try to make it to the shower before I hanged myself.

John Cheever

♦

The only *-ism* Hollywood believes in is plagiarism.

Dorothy Parker

♦

It was a hideous and untenable place when I dwelt there, populated with few exceptions by Yahoos, and now that it has become the chief citadel of television, it's unspeakable.

S.J. Perelman

♦

Hollywood money isn't money. It's congealed snow, melts in your hand, and there you are.

Dorothy Parker

Imagination and Inspiration

Like a lot of what happens in novels, inspiration is a sort of spontaneous combustion—the oily rags of the head and heart.

Stanley Elkin

♦

I've always disliked words like *inspiration*. Writing is probably like a scientist thinking about some scientific problem, or an engineer about an engineering problem.

Doris Lessing

♦

Inspiration comes out of the act of making an artifact, a work of craft.

Anthony Burgess

♦

My senses bruise easily, and when they are bruised, I write.

S.J. Perelman

Many characters have come to me...in a dream, and then I'll elaborate from there. I always write down all my dreams.
William Burroughs

◆

You never have to change anything you got up in the middle of the night to write.

Saul Bellow

◆

Only those things are beautiful which are inspired by madness and written by reason.

André Gide

◆

The devil himself always seems to get into my inkstand, and I can only exorcise him by pensful at a time.
Nathaniel Hawthorne

◆

I don't know why my imagination takes me where it does. I just feel so lucky to get a single idea for a novel that I can write about. When I get one, my ruminations and daydreaming grow and lead to other things, and I feel that there is a book there. I'm just so fortunate that I want to write it. I've never had more than one idea for a book at a time.
Joseph Heller

What stimulates me to write a poem is that I have got something inside me that I want to get rid of—it is almost a kind of defecation.

T.S. Eliot

♦

If I get a promising idea I set it down, and it stays there. I don't make myself do anything with it.

Marianne Moore

♦

I am a camera with its shutter open, quite passive, recording, not thinking.

Christopher Isherwood

♦

When they come, I write them; when they don't come, I don't.

Jack Kerouac

♦

When I sit at my table to write, I never know what it's going to be till I'm under way. I trust in inspiration, which sometimes comes and sometimes doesn't. But I don't sit back waiting for it. I work *every* day.

Alberto Moravia

I listen to the voices.

William Faulkner

♦

I don't wait to be struck by lightning and don't need certain slants of light in order to write.

Toni Morrison

♦

All you have to do is close your eyes and wait for the symbols.

Tennessee Williams

♦

When I want to get going I read Faulkner. It's good because you can't write like him.

Ken Kesey

♦

I don't know anything about inspiration because I don't know what inspiration is; I've heard about it, but I never saw it.

William Faulkner

♦

The unconscious mind has a habit of asserting itself in the afternoon.

Anthony Burgess

Journalism

Journalism is literature in a hurry.

Matthew Arnold

♦

Journalism is the entertainment business.

Frank Herbert

♦

The difference between journalism and literature is that journalism is unreadable and literature is not read.

Oscar Wilde

♦

The distinction between literature and journalism is becoming blurred; but journalism gains as much as literature loses.

W.R. Inge

Literature is the art of writing something that will be read twice; journalism what will be grasped at once.

Cyril Connolly

◆

The indispensable requirement for a good newspaper: as eager to tell a lie as the truth.

Norman Mailer

◆

The art of newspaper paragraphing is to stroke a platitude until it purrs like an epigram.

Don Marquis

◆

Journalism is the ability to meet the challenge of filling space.

Rebecca West

Literature

Literature is the question minus the answer.

Roland Barthes

♦

Literature is an answer to the questions that society asks itself about itself, but this answer is almost always unexpected.

Octavio Paz

♦

All literature is gossip.

Truman Capote

♦

Remarks are not literature.

Gertrude Stein

♦

Literature is news that *stays* news.

Ezra Pound

Literature could be said to be a sort of disciplined technique for arousing certain emotions.

Iris Murdoch

♦

Literature is recognizable through its capacity to evoke more than it says.

Anthony Burgess

♦

A losing trade, I assure you, sir: literature is a drug.

George Borrow

♦

Literature is the art of writing something that will be read twice.

Cyril Connolly

♦

Works of art and literature are not an entertainment or a diversion to amuse our leisure, but the one serious and enduring achievement of mankind—the notches on the bank of an irrigation channel which record the height to which the water once rose.

Gerald Brenan

Literature is simply the appropriate use of language.
                                        Evelyn Waugh

♦

A curious thing about written literature: It is about four thousand years old, but we have no way of knowing whether four thousand years constitutes senility or the maiden blush of youth.

                                        John Barth

♦

Literature is, primarily, a chain of connections from the past to the present. It is not reinvented every morning, as some bad writers like to believe.

                                        Gore Vidal

♦

I think it can be tremendously refreshing if a creator of literature has something on his mind other than the history of literature so far. Literature should not disappear up its own asshole, so to speak.

                                        Kurt Vonnegut

♦

Literature is the orchestration of platitudes.
                                        Thornton Wilder

All of literature is a space in which a variety of writings, none of them original, blend and crash.

Roland Barthes

♦

Great Literature is simply language charged with meaning to the utmost possible degree.

George Orwell

♦

Literature always anticipates life. It does not copy it, but molds it to its purpose. The nineteenth century, as we know it, is largely an invention of Balzac.

Oscar Wilde

♦

Medicine is my lawful wife. Literature is my mistress.

Anton Chekhov

♦

Literature is an occupation in which you have to keep proving your talent to people who have none.

Jules Renard

♦

Literature thrives on taboos, just as all art thrives on technical difficulties.

Anthony Burgess

The only sensible ends of literature are, first, the pleasurable toil of writing; second, the gratification of one's family and friends; and, lastly, the solid cash.

Nathaniel Hawthorne

♦

One handles truths like dynamite. Literature is one vast hypocrisy, a giant deception, treachery. All writers have concealed more than they revealed.

Anaïs Nin

♦

The greatest masterpiece in literature is only a dictionary out of order.

Jean Cocteau

♦

Masterpieces are no more than the shipwrecked flotsam of great minds.

Marcel Proust

♦

There is nothing like literature: I lose a cow, I write about her death, and my writing pays me enough to buy another cow.

Jules Renard

In literature the ambition of a novice is to acquire the literary language; the struggle of the adept is to get rid of it.
George Bernard Shaw

♦

To a large extent, contemporary literature is shaped by writing programs in universities. It's not that the writing programs harm people. But an awful lot of people influence people who shouldn't be influencing people.... Today the kids are standing on the shoulders of midgets.
Stanley Elkin

♦

A species living under the threat of obliteration is bound to produce obliterature—and that's what we are producing.
James Thurber

♦

There is only one school of literature—that of talent.
Vladimir Nabokov

♦

Whenever I apply myself to writing, literature comes between us.

Jules Renard

Material

A writer's material is what he cares about.

John Gardner

♦

Every artist preserves deep within him a single source from which, throughout his lifetime, he draws what he is and what he says and when the source dries up the work withers and crumbles.

Albert Camus

♦

A writer uses what experience he or she has. It's the translating, though, that makes the difference.

John Irving

A novelist is stuck with his youth. We spend it without paying much attention to how it will work out as material; nevertheless, we must draw on whatever was there for the rest of our lives. Our characters may grow old with us; we may invent or omit, fantasize or distort, their younger years, but we are all stuck.

Vance Bourjaily

♦

Most of the basic material a writer works with is acquired before the age of fifteen.

Willa Cather

♦

Almost all the great writers have as their *motif,* more or less disguised, the "passage from childhood to maturity," the clash between the thrill of expectation, and the disillusioning knowledge of the truth. *Lost Illusion* is the undisclosed title of every novel.

André Maurois

♦

Every writer has certain subjects that they write about again and again, and . . . most people's books are just variations on certain themes.

Christopher Isherwood

I think one writes and rewrites the same book. I lead a character from book to book, I continue along with the same ideas. Only the angle of vision, the method, the lighting, change.

Truman Capote

◆

Mostly, we authors must repeat ourselves—that's the truth. We have two or three great moving experiences in our lives—experiences so great and moving that it doesn't seem at the time that anyone else has been caught up and pounded and dazzled and astonished and beaten and broken and rescued and illuminated and rewarded and humbled in just that way ever before.

F. Scott Fitzgerald

◆

The work of every creator is autobiography, even if he does not know it or wish it, even if his work is "abstract." It is why you cannot re-do your work.

Jean Cocteau

◆

The man who writes about himself and his own time is the only man who writes about all people and about all time.

George Bernard Shaw

In all my writing I tell the story of my life, over and over
again.

Isaac Bashevis Singer

◆

We're stuck with it in ourselves—what we can write about,
if anything; what you can make articulate; what voices you
have in your insides and in your ear.

Robert Penn Warren

◆

And because I found I had nothing else to write about, I
presented myself as a subject.

Montaigne

◆

Almost every writer will tell you that events that happened
to him before he starts writing are the most valuable to him.
Once he starts writing he seems to observe the world
through a filter.

Irwin Shaw

◆

In literature, as in love, we are astonished at what is chosen
by others.

André Maurois

Any writer is inevitably going to work with his own anxieties and desires. If the book is any good it has got to have in it the fire of a personal unconscious mind.

Iris Murdoch

♦

There are no dull subjects. There are only dull writers.

H.L. Mencken

♦

Fundamentally, all writing is about the same thing: it's about dying, about the brief flicker of time we have here, and the frustrations that it creates.

Mordecai Richler

♦

It's all right to learn things after you've written about them, but not too much ahead of time.

John Barth

♦

There should be no distinction between what we write down and what we really know.

Allen Ginsberg

I've known a few men who were delighted at the possibility that I would write about them. "Have I been around long enough to make it into a short story?" one asked.

Elizabeth Benedict

♦

The opinions of an author are wrought by the superficial accidents of circumstance.

Jorge Luis Borges

♦

It's easier to write about those you hate—just as it's easier to criticize a bad play or a bad book.

Dorothy Parker

♦

I find it impossible to write about dumb people.

Stanley Elkin

♦

I didn't invent the world I write about—it's all true.

Graham Greene

♦

I'm at the service of the material that enters me. It takes me where it wants to go.

Russell Hoban

While many things are too strange to be believed, nothing
is too strange to have happened.

Thomas Hardy

♦

You can write about *anything,* and if you write well enough,
even the reader with no intrinsic interest in the subject will
become involved.

Tracy Kidder

♦

Of all fatiguing, futile, empty trades, the worst, I suppose,
is writing about writing.

Hilaire Belloc

Money

Sir, no man but a blockhead ever wrote except for money.
Samuel Johnson

◆

Instead of marvelling with Johnson, how anything but profit should incite men to literary labour, I am rather surprised that mere emolument should induce them to labour so well.
Thomas Green

◆

Write out of love; write out of instinct; write out of reason. But always for money.

Louis Untermeyer

◆

Write without pay until somebody offers pay; if nobody offers within three years, sawing wood is what you were intended for.

Mark Twain

Money to a writer is time to write.

Frank Herbert

◆

If I had money I'd never write.

Louis-Ferdinand Céline

◆

I only write when I need the money. I hate to work. If I got enough money, I don't write. What's the sense of making it if you can't spend it?

Mickey Spillane

◆

I've never written a book because there's going to be a lot of money in it, because I know that's the surest way to take five years off your life.

Norman Mailer

◆

If they didn't pay me, I'd do it for nothing.

Laurel Goldman

The financial rewards just don't make up for the expenditure of energy, the damage to health caused by stimulants and narcotics, the fear that one's work isn't good enough. I think, if I had enough money, I'd give up writing tomorrow.
Anthony Burgess

♦

The way I've operated with publishers is that I live on the future. I take as much money as I can get for as long as I can get it, you know, a year or two years, and by the end of that time your credit begins to have holes in it, and—well, you have to come up.

Nelson Algren

♦

Starting with a very modest advance from my publisher, I rose to near-millionaire status, then plummeted to my current state of affairs, which recently saw me borrow a few dollars from my father to fix the muffler on my car—all in eight years.

Philip Caputo

♦

There is a great discovery still to be made in literature—that of paying literary men by the quantity they do not write.
Thomas Carlyle

Almost anyone can be an author; the business is to collect money and fame from this state of being.

A.A. Milne

◆

For hundreds of years, writers have been giving it away like warmhearted country girls in the big city, and it is not astonishing that their lovers (that is, the publishers) balk at giving a mink coat when a pair of nylons will do the job.

Mario Puzo

◆

I should like to see the custom introduced of readers who are pleased with a book sending the author some small cash token: anything between half-a-crown and a hundred pounds. . . . Not more than a hundred pounds— that would be bad for my character—not less than half-a-crown—that would do no good to yours.

Cyril Connolly

◆

When you are really frantic and worried about money, you find that if it's going to be a question of writing to live, why, you just damn well buckle to and do it.

Lawrence Durrell

S. J. Perelman

(1904–1979)

The dubious privilege of a freelance writer is he's given the freedom to starve anywhere.

Writing is the hardest way of earning a living, with the possible exception of wrestling alligators.

Olin Miller

♦

If writers were good businessmen, they'd have too much sense to be writers.

Irvin S. Cobb

♦

The profession of book-writing makes horse racing seem like a solid, stable business.

John Steinbeck

♦

Writing is the only profession where no one considers you ridiculous if you earn no money.

Jules Renard

♦

Modern poets write against business, but all of us write for money.

Robert Frost

Poetry has never brought me in enough money to buy shoe-strings.

William Wordsworth

♦

Poets are terribly sensitive people, and one of the things they are most sensitive about is cash.

Robert Penn Warren

♦

Money is a kind of poetry.

Wallace Stevens

♦

There's no money in poetry, but then there's no poetry in money either.

Robert Graves

♦

I'd like to have money. And I'd like to be a good writer. These two can come together, and I hope they will, but if that's too adorable, I'd rather have money.

Dorothy Parker

The advance for a book should be at least as much as the cost of the lunch at which it was discussed.

Calvin Trillin

♦

I hope you get as much pleasure reading my book as I got spending the money you paid me for it.

Dan Poynter

♦

The writings by which one can live are not the writings which themselves live.

John Stuart Mill

♦

The two most beautiful words in the English language are "Check enclosed."

Dorothy Parker

♦

Years ago, to say you were a writer was not the highest rec-ommendation to your landlord. Today, he at least hesitates before he refuses to rent you an apartment—for all he knows you may be rich.

Arthur Miller

You must not suppose, because I am a man of letters, that I ever tried to earn an honest living.

George Bernard Shaw

♦

You must avoid giving hostages to fortune, like getting an expensive wife, an expensive house, and a style of living that never lets you afford the time to take the chance to write what you wish.

Irwin Shaw

♦

Being in a garret doesn't do you any good unless you're some sort of a Keats.

Dorothy Parker

♦

I've only spent about ten per cent of my energies on writing. The other ninety per cent went to keeping my head above water.

Katherine Anne Porter

♦

For me the main pleasure of having money is being able to afford as many completely retyped drafts as I like.

Gore Vidal

Money gives one time to rewrite books until they're "done"—or abandoned.

Gore Vidal

♦

Even if I could not earn a penny from my writing, I would earn my livelihood at something else and continue to write at night.

Irving Wallace

♦

There is only one genuinely ghastly thing hack jobs do to writers, and that is to waste their precious time.

Kurt Vonnegut

♦

I never write *metropolis* for seven cents because I can get the same price for *city*. I never write *policeman* because I can get the same money for *cop*.

Mark Twain

♦

Syntax is my bread and butter.

Roy Blount, Jr.

You can survive as a writer on hustle: you get paid very little for each piece, but you write a lot of pieces. Christ, I did book reviews—I did anything. It was $85 here, $110 there—I was like Molly Bloom: "Yes I will, yes I will, yes." Whatever anybody wanted done, I did it.

Kurt Vonnegut

♦

Why is it that an inventor can sit in a room for five years with a sheet of paper and a pencil, and when he finally comes up with something, it's capital gain; but when writers do the same thing, it's current income, which is heavily taxed?

Adam Smith

Motives and Aspirations

The writer has a grudge against society, which he documents with accounts of unsatisfying sex, unrealized ambition, unmitigated loneliness, and a sense of local and global distress.

Renata Adler

♦

Every author really wants to have letters printed in the papers. Unable to make the grade, he drops down a rung of the ladder and writes novels.

P.G. Wodehouse

♦

I do think that the quality which makes a man want to write and be read is essentially a desire for self-exposure and is masochistic. Like one of those guys who has a compulsion to take his thing out and show it on the street.

James Jones

Writing a book is such a complicated, long-term, difficult process that all of the possible motives that can funnel in will, and a great many of those motives will be base. If you can transform your particular baseness into something beautiful, that's about the best you can make of your own obnoxious nature.

William Gass

♦

Writers, if they are worthy of that jealous designation, do not write for other writers. They write to give reality to experience.

Archibald MacLeish

♦

All writers are vain, selfish, and lazy, and at the very bottom of their motives there lies a mystery. Writing a book is a horrible, exhausting struggle, like a long bout of some painful illness. One would never undertake such a thing if one were not driven on by some demon whom one can neither resist nor understand. For all one knows that demon is simply the same instinct that makes a baby squall for attention.

George Orwell

There are three reasons for becoming a writer: the first is that you need the money; the second, that you have something to say that you think the world should know; the third is that you can't think what to do with the long winter evenings.

Quentin Crisp

♦

Why had I become a writer in the first place? Because I wasn't fit for society; I didn't fit into the system.

Brian Aldiss

♦

I write to ease the passing of time.

Jorge Luis Borges

♦

The number one reason why any professional writer writes is to pay the bills. This isn't the Lawn Tennis Association where you play just for the thrill of it.

Jimmy Breslin

♦

I write because I hate. A lot. Hard.

William Gass

♦

I write books to find out about things.

Rebecca West

They ask me if I were on a desert island and knew nobody would ever see what I wrote, would I go on writing. My answer is most emphatically yes, I would go on writing for company. Because I'm creating an imaginary—it's always imaginary—world in which I would like to live.

William Burroughs

♦

I'm not one of those writers you'll hear say, "When you are a writer, you never retire, you go on writing—that's your life." Living is my life. I write in order to stay alive.

Quentin Crisp

♦

I feel a need to have a certain experience, to see certain feelings displayed, to see certain ideas pursued, and at one point or another I make the audacious choice of appointing myself as the person who can conceivably do that.

Scott Spencer

♦

I started writing because of a terrible feeling of powerlessness: I felt I was drifting and obscure, and I rebelled against that. I didn't see what I could do to change my condition. I wanted to control rather than be controlled, to ordain rather than be ordained, and to relegate rather than be relegated.

Anita Brookner

I revel in the prospect of being able to torture a phrase once more.

S.J. Perelman

◆

How do I know what I think until I see what I say?

E.M. Forster

◆

Writers write to influence their readers, their preachers, their auditors, but always, at bottom, to be more themselves.

Aldous Huxley

◆

There are many reasons why novelists write, but they all have one thing in common: a need to create an alternative world.

John Fowles

◆

My purpose is to entertain myself first and other people secondly.

John D. MacDonald

◆

I write in order to attain that feeling of tension relieved and function achieved which a cow enjoys on giving milk.

H.L. Mencken

The only reason for being a professional writer is that you just can't help it.

Leo Rosten

♦

I have always been in a condition in which I cannot *not* write.
Barbara Tuchman

♦

I can say now that one of the big reasons was this: I instinctively recognized an opportunity to transcend some of my personal failings—things about myself I didn't particularly like and wanted to change but didn't know how.

John Steinbeck

♦

I write fiction because it's a way of making statements I can disown. I write plays because dialogue is the most respectable way of contradicting myself.

Tom Stoppard

♦

The physical business of writing is unpleasant to me, but the psychic satisfaction of discharging bad ideas in worse English makes me forget it.

H.L. Mencken

One writes to find words' meanings.

Joy Williams

♦

Getting even is one reason for writing.

William Gass

♦

If you ask me what I came to do in this world, I, an artist, I will answer you: I am here to live out loud.

Émile Zola

♦

I shall live badly if I do not write, and I shall write badly if I do not live.

Françoise Sagan

♦

If I could think, maybe I wouldn't write.

Scott Spencer

♦

My main reason for adopting literature as a profession was that, as the author is never seen by his clients, he need not dress respectably.

George Bernard Shaw

William Faulkner

(1897–1962)

All of us failed to match our dreams of perfection.

A writer is someone who writes, that's all. You can't stop it; you can't make yourself do anything else but that.

Gore Vidal

♦

I love to tell stories.

Irving Wallace

♦

The writer's intention hasn't anything to do with what he achieves. The intent to earn money or the intent to be famous or the intent to be great doesn't matter in the end. Just what comes out.

Lillian Hellman

♦

I wrote a short story because I wanted to see something of mine in print, other than my fingers.

Wilson Mizner

♦

I wrote my first novel because I wanted to read it.

Toni Morrison

♦

At the time of writing, I don't write for my friends or myself, either; I write for *it*, for the pleasure of *it*.

Eudora Welty

If you can't annoy somebody, there is little point in writing.
Kingsley Amis

♦

On the whole, I don't want to think too much about why I write what I write. If I know what I'm doing. . . I can't do it.
Joan Didion

♦

What I am trying to achieve is a voice sitting by a fireplace telling you a story on a winter's evening.

Truman Capote

♦

Unless one is a genius, it is best to aim at being intelligible.
Anthony Hope Hawkins

♦

A writer's problem does not change. He himself changes and the world he lives in changes but his problem remains the same. It is always how to write truly and having found what is true, to project it in such a way that it becomes part of the experience of the person who reads it.

Ernest Hemingway

Any writer overwhelmingly honest about pleasing himself is almost sure to please others.

Marianne Moore

♦

I never wanted to grow up to be a writer, I just wanted to grow up to be an adult.

Toni Morrison

♦

I never deliberately set out to shock, but when people don't walk out of my plays I think there is something wrong.

John Osborne

♦

The sour truth is that I am imprisoned with a perception which will settle for nothing less than making a revolution in the consciousness of our time.

Norman Mailer

♦

Anything that is written to please the author is worthless.

Blaise Pascal

The writer who aims at producing the platitudes which are "not for an age but for all time" has his reward in being unreadable in all ages.

George Bernard Shaw

◆

A good writer always works at the impossible.

John Steinbeck

◆

I am trying—in a good cause—to crowd people out of their own minds and occupy their space. I want them to stop being themselves for the moment, I want them to stop thinking, and I want to occupy their heads. I want to use language and I want the language to reverberate and I want to use the white spaces between the lines.

Robert Stone

◆

What I want to do is make people laugh so they'll see things seriously.

William Zinsser

◆

I want to be the Minnesota Fats of science fiction.

Frank Herbert

I intend to become America's black female Proust.

Maya Angelou

♦

I have tried simply to write the best I can; sometimes I have good luck and write better than I can.

Ernest Hemingway

♦

A book is produced by the whole man, who is more complicated than any other single object in the universe, and its motivation is therefore just as mysterious and ineluctable.

William Golding

♦

I always wanted to write a book that ended with the word *mayonnaise*.

Richard Brautigan

Novels and Novelists

*N*ovel, *n.* A short story padded.

Ambrose Bierce

♦

A novel is a mirror walking along a main road.

Stendhal

♦

A novel is never anything but a philosophy put into images.

Albert Camus

♦

The novel is rescued life.

Hortense Calisher

♦

A novel is a prose narrative of some length that has something wrong with it.

Randall Jarrell

The novel is an unknown man and I have to find him.

Graham Greene

◆

The novel is the highest example of subtle interrelatedness that man has discovered.

D.H. Lawrence

◆

The novel is a game or joke shared between author and reader.

Annie Dillard

◆

All novels are experimental.

Anthony Burgess

◆

A good novel tells us the truth about its hero; but a bad novel tells us the truth about its author.

G.K. Chesterton

◆

When we want to understand grief beyond grief, or the eternal confrontation of man and woman, man and God, man and himself, we go to the novel.

Richard Condon

To me a novel is something that's built around the character of time, the nature of time, and the effects that time has on events and characters. When I see a novel that's supposed to take place in twenty-four hours, I just wonder why the man padded out the short story.

Frank O'Connor

♦

The novel is practically a Protestant form of art; it is a product of the free mind, of the autonomous individual.

George Orwell

♦

Every novel worthy of the name is like another planet, whether large or small, which has its own laws just as it has its own flora and fauna.

François Mauriac

♦

I view the novel, a single novel as well as a writer's entire corpus, as a musical composition in which the characters are themes, from variation to variation completing an entire parabola; similarly for the themes themselves.

Alberto Moravia

The novel is something that never was before and will not be again.

Eudora Welty

♦

Secrets. Need to disguise. The novel was born of this.

Anaïs Nin

♦

What is a novel but a universe in which action is endowed with form, where final words are pronounced, where people possess one another completely and where life assumes the aspect of destiny?

Albert Camus

♦

Human beings have their great chance in the novel.

E.M. Forster

♦

Reading about imaginary characters and their adventures is the greatest pleasure in the world. Or the second greatest.

Anthony Burgess

♦

The love of novels is the preference of sentiment to the senses.

Ralph Waldo Emerson

Virginia Woolf

(1882–1941)

Nothing induces me to read a novel except when I have to make money by writing about it. I detest them.

Reading novels—serious novels, anyhow—is an experience limited to a very small percentage of the so-called enlightened public. Increasingly, it's going to be a pursuit for those who seek unusual experiences, moral fetishists perhaps, people of heightened imagination, the troubled pursuers of the ambiguous self.

Jerzy Kosinski

◆

It is the sexless novel that should be distinguished: the sex novel is now normal.

George Bernard Shaw

◆

The American novel is a conquest of the frontier; as it describes experience it creates it.

Ralph Ellison

◆

I miss the spirit of social activism in American literature of the '20s and '30s. In your novels I learn a lot about universities and teachers. They are well written, but they bore me.

Günter Grass

All modern American literature comes from one book by Mark Twain called *Huckleberry Finn*.

Ernest Hemingway

♦

One should not be too severe on English novels; they are the only relaxation of the intellectually unemployed.

Oscar Wilde

♦

A good novel is possible only after one has given up and let go.

Walker Percy

♦

The real comic novel has to do with man's recognition of his unimportance in the universe.

Anthony Burgess

♦

The serious novel is now almost in the same situation as poetry. Eventually the novel will simply be an academic exercise, written by academics to be used in classrooms in order to test the ingenuity of students.

Gore Vidal

I did not begin to write novels until I had forgotten all I had learned at school and college.

John Galsworthy

♦

There are three rules for writing a novel. Unfortunately, no one knows what they are.

W. Somerset Maugham

♦

There are no laws for the novel. There never have been, nor can there be.

Doris Lessing

♦

One is improvising when one writes, and you pick up in the same way a musician starts to improvise and detect the inner structure of what he's playing—that's the way I think it works in the writing of a novel. You pick up the beat.

Robert Stone

♦

One ought to know a lot about reality before one writes realistic novels.

John Barth

It's important that a novel be approached with some urgency. Spend too long on it, or have great gaps between writing sessions, and the unity of the work tends to be lost.

Anthony Burgess

♦

A novel has to limit itself to the crew of a ship or a family; it's not a great way to process a huge number of people.

Kurt Vonnegut

♦

In any work that is truly creative, I believe, the writer cannot be omniscient in advance about the effects that he proposes to produce. The suspense of a novel is not only in the reader, but in the novelist, who is intensely curious about what will happen to the hero.

Mary McCarthy

♦

The human race needs the novel. We need all the experience we can get. Those who say the novel is dead can't write them.

Bernard Malamud

I would sooner read a time-table or a catalogue than nothing at all. . . . They are much more entertaining than half the novels that are written.

W. Somerset Maugham

♦

A novelist is a person who lives in other people's skins.

E.L. Doctorow

♦

A novelist is the only writer who can make a name without a style, which is only one more reason for not bothering with the novel.

Robert Frost

♦

The novelist is a shaman who is. . .offering his experience for the use of the rest of the tribe.

Russell Hoban

♦

The novelist is, above all, the historian of conscience.

Frederic Raphael

The complete novelist would come into the world with a catalog of qualities something like this. He would own the concentration of a Trappist monk, the organizational ability of a Prussian field marshal, the insight into human relations of a Viennese psychiatrist, the discipline of a man who prints the Lord's Prayer on the head of a pin, the exquisite sense of timing of an Olympic gymnast, and by the way, a natural instinct and flair for exceptional use of language.

Leon Uris

♦

They can't yank a novelist like they can a pitcher. A novelist has to go the full nine, even if it kills him.

Ernest Hemingway

♦

A novelist must preserve a child-like belief in the importance of things which common sense considers of no great consequence.

W. Somerset Maugham

♦

The stage conjuror is perhaps the only other person permitted to play havoc with the minds of his audience and not be resented.

Len Deighton

Unfortunately, thrashing your young woman doesn't make her admire you more as a novelist.

William Cooper

◆

I suppose I am a born novelist, for the things I imagine are more vital and vivid to me than the things I remember.

Ellen Glasgow

◆

It is a fact that few novelists enjoy the creative labour, though most enjoy thinking about the creative labour.

Arnold Bennett

◆

I am a man, and alive...For this reason I am a novelist. And being a novelist, I consider myself superior to the saint, the scientist, the philosopher, and the poet, who are all great masters of different bits of man alive, but never get the whole hog.

D.H. Lawrence

◆

As artists, women novelists are rot, but as providers they are oil wells—they gush.

Dorothy Parker

Unlike God, the novelist does not start with nothing and make something of it. He starts with himself as nothing and makes something of the nothing with the things at hand.

Walker Percy

♦

The novelist is dead in the man who has become aware of the triviality of human affairs.

W. Somerset Maugham

♦

Most writers are not quick-witted when they talk. Novelists, in particular, drag themselves around in society like gut-shot bears.

Kurt Vonnegut

Originality

Originality is nothing but judicious imitation. The most original writers borrowed from one another. The instruction we find in books is like fire. We fetch it from our neighbors, kindle it at home, communicate it to others, and it becomes the property of all.

Voltaire

♦

Everything has been thought of before, but the problem is to think of it again.

Goethe

♦

Who is original? Everything that we are doing, everything that we think, exists already, and we are only intermediaries, that's all, who make use of what is in the air.

Henry Miller

About the most originality that any writer can hope to achieve honestly is to steal with good judgment.

Josh Billings

◆

A sequel is an admission that you've been reduced to imitating yourself.

Don Marquis

◆

Casting my mind's eye over the whole of fiction, the only absolutely original creation I can think of is *Don Quixote*.

W. Somerset Maugham

◆

An original writer is not one who imitates nobody, but one whom nobody can imitate.

Francois-René de Châteaubriand

◆

Derivative writers seem versatile because they imitate many others, past and present. Artistic originality has only itself to copy.

Vladimir Nabokov

He has left off reading altogether to the great improvement of his originality.

Charles Lamb

♦

Originality does not consist in saying what no one has ever said before, but in saying exactly what you think yourself.

J.F. Stephen

♦

The original writer, as long as he isn't dead, is always scandalous.

Simone de Beauvoir

♦

Originality is undetected plagiarism.

William Inge

♦

If Thomas Wolfe sold, I'd write like Thomas Wolfe.

Mickey Spillane

Output

I wrote much because I was paid little.

Anthony Burgess

♦

[I'm] a sausage machine, a perfect machine.

Agatha Christie

♦

I have the conviction that excessive literary production is a social offense.

George Eliot

♦

Wearing down seven number two pencils is a good day's work.

Ernest Hemingway

Three hours a day will produce as much as a man ought to write.

Anthony Trollope

◆

Two thousand words a day is very good going.

Evelyn Waugh

◆

If my doctor told me I had only six months to live, I wouldn't brood. I'd type a little faster.

Isaac Asimov

◆

Only a small minority of authors over-write themselves. Most of the good and the tolerable ones do not write enough.

Arnold Bennett

◆

Unlike Andy Rooney, who puts out a book every year, I at least have the courtesy to wait two years before I offer something new.

Art Buchwald

◆

I'm a commercial writer, not an "author." Margaret Mitchell was an author. She wrote one book.

Mickey Spillane

Nine out of ten writers, I am sure, could write more. I think they should and, if they did, they would find their work improving even beyond their own, their agent's, and their editor's highest hopes.

John Creasey

♦

Looking back, I imagine I was always writing. Twaddle it was, too. But better far write twaddle or anything, anything, than nothing at all.

Katherine Mansfield

♦

If you have one strong idea, you can't help repeating it and embroidering it. Sometimes I think that authors should write one book and then be put in a gas chamber.

John P. Marquand

♦

I can't turn out slews of stuff each day. I wish I could. I seem to have some neurotic need to perfect each paragraph—each sentence, even—as I go along.

William Styron

♦

The less you write, the better it must be.

Jules Renard

Plagiarism

Whatever has been well said by anyone is mine.

Seneca

♦

The difference between a bad artist and a good one is: The bad artist seems to copy a great deal; the good one really does.

William Blake

♦

Good swiping is an art in itself.

Jules Feiffer

♦

The Eighth Commandment was not made for bards.

Samuel Taylor Coleridge

No man ever yet became great by imitation.

Samuel Johnson

♦

Immature artists imitate. Mature artists steal.

Lionel Trilling

♦

The immature poet imitates; the mature poet plagiarizes.

T.S. Eliot

♦

It has come to be practically a sort of rule in literature, that a man, having once shown himself capable of original writing, is entitled thenceforth to steal from the writings of others at discretion.

Ralph Waldo Emerson

♦

When a thing has been said and well said, have no scruple; take it and copy it. Give references? Why should you? Either your readers know where you have taken the passage and the precaution is needless, or they do not know and you humiliate them.

Anatole France

Though old the thought and oft exprest,
'Tis his at last who says it best.

James Russell Lowell

♦

Another illusion, seldom entertained by competent authors, is that the publisher's readers and others are waiting to plagiarize their work. I think it may be said that the more worthless the manuscript, the greater the fear of plagiarism.

Stanley Unwin

♦

Next o'er his books his eyes began to roll,
In pleasing memory of all he stole.

Alexander Pope

♦

Plagiarists are always suspicious of being stolen from.

Samuel Taylor Coleridge

♦

They lard their lean books with the fat of others' work.

Robert Burton

♦

Taking something from one man and making it worse is plagiarism.

George Moore

Robert Benchley

(1889–1945)

Great literature must spring from an upheaval in the author's soul. If that upheaval is not present, then it must come from the works of any other author which happen to be handy and easily adapted.

When a man's talk is commonplace and his writings uncommon, it means that his talent lies in the place from which he borrows it, and not in himself.

Montaigne

♦

It is a mean thief, or a successful author, that plunders the dead.

Austin O'Malley

♦

Every man is a borrower and a mimic, life is theatrical and literature a quotation.

Ralph Waldo Emerson

♦

Steal! And egad, serve your best thoughts as gypsies do stolen children, disfigure them to make 'em pass for their own.

Richard Brinsley Sheridan

♦

Adam was the only man who, when he said a good thing, knew that nobody had said it before him.

Mark Twain

Truth and reason are common to all and no more belong to him that spoke them heretofore than unto him that shall speak them hereafter.

Montaigne

♦

When 'Omer smote 'is bloomin' lyre,
  He'd 'eard men sing by land and sea;
An' what 'e thought 'e might require,
  'E went an' took—the same as me!

Rudyard Kipling

♦

Nothing is new except arrangement.

Will Durant

♦

I do borrow from other writers, *shamelessly!* I can only say in my defense, like the woman brought before the judge on a charge of kleptomania, "I do steal; but, Your Honor, only from the very best stores."

Thornton Wilder

♦

I pinch.

Lawrence Durrell

Poets and Poetry

The poet is like the prince of the clouds, who rides the tempest and scorns the archer. Exiled on the ground, amidst boos and insults, his giant's wings prevent his walking.

Charles Baudelaire

♦

A taste for drawing rooms has spoiled more poets than ever did a taste for gutters.

Thomas Beer

♦

Poets have to dream, and dreaming in America is no cinch.

Saul Bellow

♦

A famous poet is a discoverer, rather than an inventor.

Jorge Luis Borges

Modesty is a virtue not often found among poets, for almost every one of them thinks himself the greatest in the world.

Cervantes

♦

True poets should be chaste, I know,
But wherefore should their lines be so?

Catullus

♦

The poet is a liar who always speaks the truth.

Jean Cocteau

♦

Anyone may be an honorable man, and yet write verse badly.

Molière

♦

Turn pimp, flatterer, quack, lawyer, parson, be chaplain to an atheist, or stallion to an old woman, anything but a poet; for a poet is worse, more servile, timorous and fawning than any I have named.

William Congreve

A poet, with the exception of mysterious water-fluent tea-drinking *Auden,* must be a highly-conscious technical expert.
Cyril Connolly

♦

True poets are the guardians of the state.
Wentworth Dillon

♦

To become a poet is to take the whole field of human knowledge and human desire for one's province...but this field can only be covered by continual inner abdications.
Lawrence Durrell

♦

A poet can survive anything but a misprint.
Oscar Wilde

♦

In the case of many poets, the most important thing for them to do...is to write as little as possible.
T.S. Eliot

An unromantic poet is a self-contradiction, like the democratic aristocrat that reads the *Atlantic Monthly*.

Robert Frost

♦

The public has an unusual relation with the poet. It does not even know that he is there.

Randall Jarrell

♦

The poet is the rock of defense for human nature.

William Wordsworth

♦

Poets die in different ways: most of them do not die into the grave, but into business or criticism.

Robert Frost

♦

Poets have gotten so careless, it's a disgrace. You can't pick up a page. All the words slide off.

William Gass

♦

Poets have to learn karate, these days.

Yevgeny Yevtushenko

Buffoons and poets are near related
And willingly seek each other out.

Goethe

♦

Nine-tenths of English poetic literature is the result either
of vulgar careerism, or of a poet trying to keep his hand in.
Most poets are dead by their late twenties.

Robert Graves

♦

Poets are like baseball pitchers. Both have their moments.
The intervals are the tough things.

Robert Frost

♦

To be a poet is a condition rather than a profession.

Robert Graves

♦

Poets don't have an "audience." They're talking to a single
person all the time.

Robert Graves

Democritus maintains that there can be no great poet without a spice of madness.

Cicero

♦

The man is either crazy or he is a poet.

Horace

♦

The courage of the poet is to keep ajar the door that leads into madness.

Christopher Morley

♦

Perhaps no person can be a poet, or can even enjoy poetry, without a certain unsoundness of mind.

Thomas Babington Macaulay

♦

All poets are mad.

Robert Burton

♦

It seems that God took away the minds of poets that they might better express His.

Socrates

No wonder poets sometimes have to *seem*
So much more business-like than business men.
Their wares are so much harder to get rid of.

Robert Frost

◆

Poets were the first teachers of mankind.

Horace

◆

Lyric poets generally come from homes run by women.

Milan Kundera

◆

No honest poet can ever feel quite sure of the permanent
value of what he has written: he may have wasted his time
and messed up his life for nothing.

T.S. Eliot

◆

Poets are born, not paid.

Wilson Mizner

◆

The bad poet is usually unconscious where he ought to be
conscious, and conscious where he ought to be unconscious.

T.S. Eliot

I'd rather be a great bad poet than a good bad poet.

Ogden Nash

♦

No bad man can be a good poet.

Boris Pasternak

♦

All poets who, when reading from their own works, experience a choked feeling, are major. For that matter, all poets who read from their own works are major, whether they choke or not.

E.B. White

♦

The poet is the unsatisfied child who dares to ask the difficult question which arises from the schoolmaster's answer to his simple question, and then the still more difficult question which arises from that.

Robert Graves

♦

A poet more than thirty years old is simply an overgrown child.

H.L. Mencken

When one hears of a poet past thirty-five, he seems some-how unnatural and even a trifle obscene; it is as if one en-countered a greying man who still played the Chopin waltzes and believed in elective affinities.

H.L. Mencken

♦

Poets are almost always bald when they get to be about forty.

John Masefield

♦

A poet should be treated with leniency and, even when damned, should be damned with respect.

Edgar Allan Poe

♦

Sir, I admit your general rule,
That every poet is a fool;
But you yourself may serve to show it,
That every fool is not a poet.

Alexander Pope

♦

Poets aren't very useful.
Because they aren't consumeful or very produceful.

Ogden Nash

My quarrel with poets is not that they are unclear, but that they are too diligent.

E.B. White

♦

No man can be explained by his personal history, least of all a poet.

Katherine Anne Porter

♦

Poets are the unacknowledged legislators of the world.

Percy Bysshe Shelley

♦

War talk by men who have been in a war is interesting, but moon talk by a poet who has not been in the moon is dull.

Mark Twain

♦

Poets alone are permitted to tell the real truth.

Horace Walpole

♦

The poet marries the language, and out of this marriage the poem is born.

W.H. Auden

Today's poet has less trouble making himself heard than making himself plain.

Louis Untermeyer

♦

A poet dares to be just so clear and no clearer; he approaches lucid ground warily, like a mariner who is determined not to scrape his bottom on anything solid. A poet's pleasure is to withhold a little of his meaning, to intensify by mystification. He unzips the veil from beauty, but does not remove it. A poet utterly clear is a trifle glaring.

E.B. White

♦

As a poet, there is only one political duty, and that is to defend one's language from corruption.

W.H. Auden

♦

The poet is the priest of the invisible.

Wallace Stevens

Isak Dinesen

(1885–1962)

A poet's mission is to make others confound fiction and reality in order to render them, for an hour, mysteriously happy.

Like a piece of ice on a hot stove the poem must ride on its own melting.

Robert Frost

♦

Information is true if it is accurate. A poem is true if it holds together.

E.M. Forster

♦

A poem begins in delight and ends in wisdom.

Robert Frost

♦

Poetry is like fish: if it's fresh, it's good; if it's stale, it's bad; and if you're not certain, try it on the cat.

Osbert Sitwell

♦

All bad poetry springs from genuine feeling.

Oscar Wilde

♦

I should define a good poem as one that makes complete sense; and says all it has to say memorably and economically, and has been written for no other than poetic reasons.

Robert Graves

A perfect poem is impossible. Once it had been written, the world would end.

Robert Graves

♦

It is easier to write a mediocre poem than to understand a good one.

Montaigne

♦

The poem is not made from these letters that I drive in like nails, but of the white which remains on the paper.

Paul Claudel

♦

The only really difficult thing about a poem is the critic's explanation of it.

Frank Moore Colby

♦

When you read and understand a poem, comprehending its rich and formal meanings, then you master chaos a little.

Stephen Spender

♦

Poetry is what gets lost in translation.

Robert Frost

In a poem the words should be as pleasing to the ear as the meaning is to the mind.

Marianne Moore

♦

If it were not for poetry, few men would ever fall in love.
La Rochefoucauld

♦

Love poems must be bounced back off a moon.
Robert Graves

♦

Of our conflicts with others we make rhetoric; of our conflicts with ourselves we make poetry.

William Butler Yeats

♦

Poetry is more philosophical and of higher value than history.

Aristotle

♦

Too many people in the modern world view poetry as a luxury, not a necessity, like petrol.

John Betjeman

In poetry you have a form looking for a subject and a subject looking for a form. When they come together successfully you have a poem.

W.H. Auden

♦

Perfect things in poetry do not seem strange, they seem inevitable.

Jorge Luis Borges

♦

A poem should not mean, but be.

Archibald MacLeish

♦

Poetry is what Milton saw when he went blind.

Don Marquis

♦

Poetry is the deification of reality.

Edith Sitwell

♦

Poetry is the result of a struggle in the poet's mind between something he wants to say and the medium in which he is trying to say it.

Gerald Brenan

I know that poetry is indispensable, but to what I could
not say.

Jean Cocteau

♦

If I feel physically as if the top of my head were taken off,
I know that is poetry.

Emily Dickinson

♦

Poetry is not an assertion of truth, but the making of that
truth more fully real to us.

T.S. Eliot

♦

Poetry is ordinary language raised to the nth degree.

Paul Engle

♦

Poetry's a mere drug, Sir.

George Farquhar

♦

True poetry makes things happen.

Robert Graves

Poetry is a mug's game.

T.S. Eliot

♦

Poetry is the impish attempt to paint the color of the wind.
Maxwell Bodenheim

♦

Poetry is the synthesis of hyacinths and biscuits.

Carl Sandburg

♦

If a line of poetry strays into my memory, my skin bristles
so that the razor ceases to act.

A.E. Housman

♦

Poetry is the only art people haven't yet learned to consume
like soup.

W.H. Auden

♦

Even when poetry has a meaning, as it usually has, it may
be inadvisable to draw it out. . . . Perfect understanding will
sometimes always extinguish pleasure.

A.E. Housman

Poetry is trouble dunked in tears.

Gwyn Thomas

♦

Poetry is the bill and coo of sex.

Elbert Hubbard

♦

Poetry is life distilled.

Gwendolyn Brooks

♦

Poetry is the journal of a sea animal living on land, wanting to fly in the air.

Carl Sandburg

♦

All poetry is putting the infinite with the finite.

Robert Browning

♦

Literature is a state of culture, poetry is a state of grace.

Juan Ramón Jiménez

♦

Poetry is the art of uniting pleasure with truth.

Samuel Johnson

Boswell: Then, Sir, what is poetry?
Johnson: Why, Sir, it is much easier to say what it is not. We
all *know* what light is; but it is not easy to *tell* what it is.
                                        Boswell's Life of Johnson

◆

Poetry is a report of some human experience ordered in
terms of concepts involving a value judgment.
                                        Joseph Wood Krutch

◆

Two poetries are now competing, a cooked and a raw. The
cooked, marvelously expert, often seems laboriously con-
cocted to be tasted and digested by a graduate seminar. The
raw, huge, blood-dripping gobbets of unseasoned experience
are dished up for midnight listeners.

                                        Robert Lowell

◆

I think that one possible definition of our modern culture
is that it is one in which nine-tenths of our intellectuals can't
read any poetry.

                                        Randall Jarrell

If poetry comes not as naturally as the leaves to a tree, it had better not come at all.

John Keats

♦

Indifference to poetry is one of the most conspicuous characteristics of the human race.

Robert S. Lynd

♦

If left to its own tendencies, I believe poetry would exclude everything but love and the moon.

Robert Frost

♦

Poetry is the search for syllables to shoot at the barriers of the unknown and the unknowable.

Carl Sandburg

♦

You will not find poetry anywhere unless you bring some of it with you.

Joseph Joubert

♦

Poetry is the art of understanding what it is to be alive.
Archibald MacLeish

The crown of literature is poetry. It is its end aim. It is the sublimest activity of the human mind. It is the achievement of beauty and delicacy. The writer of prose can only step aside when the poet passes.

W. Somerset Maugham

♦

To write good prose is an affair of good manners. It is, unlike verse, a civil art.... Poetry is baroque.

W. Somerset Maugham

♦

Poetry, surely, is a crisis, perhaps the only actionable one we can call our own.

J.D. Salinger

♦

Poetry is all nouns and verbs.

Marianne Moore

♦

Poetry...the mysteries of the irrational perceived through rational words.

Vladimir Nabokov

Poetry is language surprised in the act of changing into meaning.

Stanley Kunitz

◆

My verse represents a handle I can grasp in order not to yield to the centrifugal forces which are trying to throw me off the world.

Ogden Nash

◆

Poetry is the revelation of a feeling that the poet believes to be interior and personal which the reader recognizes as his own.

Salvatore Quasimodo

◆

Lying of an inspired, habitual, inventive kind, given a personality, a form, and a rhythm, is mainly what poetry is.

James Dickey

◆

Poetry is adolescence fermented, and thus preserved.

José Ortega y Gasset

The blood jet is poetry
There is no stopping it.

Sylvia Plath

♦

Poetry is the renewal of words, setting them free, and that's
what a poet is doing: loosening the words.

Robert Frost

♦

Poetry is fact given over to imagery.

Rod McKuen

♦

Poetry is a way of taking life by the throat.

Robert Frost

♦

Poetry is the rhythmical creation of beauty in words.
Edgar Allan Poe

♦

A beautiful line of verse has twelve feet, and two wings.
Jules Renard

I have no fancy ideas about poetry. It doesn't come to you on the wings of a dove. It's something you work hard at.

Louise Bogan

♦

If . . . it makes my whole body so cold no fire can warm me, I know that is poetry.

Emily Dickinson

♦

Poetry is a comforting piece of fiction set to more or less lascivious music.

H.L. Mencken

♦

Poetry is the presentment in musical form to the imagination, of noble grounds for the noble emotions.

John Ruskin

♦

I am overwhelmed by the beautiful disorder of poetry, the eternal virginity of words.

Theodore Roethke

♦

I've written some poetry I don't understand myself.

Carl Sandburg

Poetry is a spot about half-way between where you listen
and where you wonder what it was you heard.

Carl Sandburg

♦

Poetry is the silence and speech between a wet struggling
root of a flower and sunlit blossom of that flower.

Carl Sandburg

♦

Poetry is the opening and closing of a door, leaving those
who look through to guess about what was seen during a
moment.

Carl Sandburg

♦

Poetry is what makes the invisible appear.

Nathalie Sarraute

♦

Poetry is a religion without hope.

Jean Cocteau

♦

Poetry is the spontaneous overflow of powerful feelings; it
takes its origin from emotion recollected in tranquility.

William Wordsworth

Poetry is the record of the best and happiest moments of the happiest and best minds.

Percy Bysshe Shelley

♦

Poetry and consumption are the most flattering of diseases.

William Shenstone

♦

Great poetry is always written by somebody straining to go beyond what he can do.

Stephen Spender

♦

Poetry is the mathematics of writing and closely kin to music.

John Steinbeck

♦

Ignorance is one of the sources of poetry.

Wallace Stevens

♦

I could no more define poetry than a terrier can define a rat.

A.E. Housman

I like to think of poetry as statements made on the way to the grave.

Dylan Thomas

For me, poetry is an evasion of the real job of writing prose.
Sylvia Plath

I wish our clever young poets would remember my homely definitions of prose and poetry; that is, prose—words in their best order; poetry—the best words in their best order.
Samuel Taylor Coleridge

Poetry is better understood in the verse of the artist than in the prose of the critic.

Matthew Arnold

Poetry is to prose as dancing is to walking.

John Wain

Poetry is simply the most beautiful, impressive, and widely effective mode of saying things.

Matthew Arnold

Poetry is mostly hunches.

John Ashbery

♦

Poetry is the breath and finer spirit of all knowledge; it is the impassioned expression which is in the countenance of all Science.

William Wordsworth

♦

Poetry provides the one permissible way of saying one thing and meaning another.

Robert Frost

♦

Blank verse, n. Unrhymed iambic pentameters—the most difficult kind of English verse to write acceptably; a kind, therefore, much affected by those who cannot acceptably write any kind.

Ambrose Bierce

♦

Free verse is like free love; it is a contradiction in terms.

G.K. Chesterton

Writing free verse is like playing tennis with the net down.
Robert Frost

♦

No *vers* is *libre* for the man who wants to do a good job.
T.S. Eliot

♦

The writers of free verse got their idea from incorrect proof pages.

Robert Frost

Posterity

A falsehood once received from a famed writer becomes traditional to posterity.

John Dryden

♦

Posterity—what you write for after being turned down by publishers.

George Ade

♦

I don't care about posterity. I'm writing for today.

Kurt Weill

♦

When a man is in doubt about this or that in his writing, it will often guide him if he asks himself how it will tell a hundred years hence.

Samuel Butler

To invoke one's posterity is to make a speech to maggots.
Louis-Ferdinand Céline

♦

When I am dead, I hope it may be said:
"His sins were scarlet, but his books were read."
Hilaire Belloc

Postpartum

Finishing a book is just like you took a child out in the yard and shot it.

Truman Capote

♦

For a dyed-in-the-wool author nothing is so dead as a book once it is written...she is rather like a cat whose kittens have grown up.

Rumer Godden

♦

When a book is done, he has his own life and you forget about him. He goes and lives alone; he takes an apartment.

Oriana Fallaci

The book dies a real death for me when I write the last word. I have a little sorrow and then go on to a new book which is alive. The rows of my books on the shelf are to me like very well embalmed corpses. They are neither alive nor mine. I have no sorrow for them because I have forgotten them, forgotten in its truest sense.

John Steinbeck

♦

I usually have a sense of clinical fatigue after finishing a book.
John Cheever

♦

Writing every book is like a purge; at the end of it one is empty. . .like a dry shell on the beach, waiting for the tide to come in again.

Daphne du Maurier

♦

I truly do not care about a book once it is finished. Any money or fame that results has no connection with my feelings with the book.

John Steinbeck

I don't keep any copy of my books around . . . . They would embarrass me. When I finish writing my books, I kick them in the belly, and have done with them.

Ludwig Bemelmans

♦

I scarcely look with full satisfaction upon any; for they do not seem what they might have been. I often wish that I could have twenty years more, to take them down from the shelf one by one, and write them over.

Washington Irving

Process

I write the big scenes first, that is, the scenes that carry the meaning of the book, the emotional experience.

Joyce Cary

◆

The pattern of the thing precedes the thing. I fill in the gaps of the crossword at any spot I happen to choose. These bits I write on index cards until the novel is done.

Vladimir Nabokov

◆

I write any sort of rubbish which will cover the main outlines of the story, then I can begin to see it.

Frank O'Connor

I do not write and never have written to an arranged plot. The book is composed at once like a picture, and may start anywhere, in the middle or at the end. I may go from the end to the beginning in the same day, and then from the beginning to the middle.

Joyce Cary

◆

As for my next book, I am going to hold myself from writing it till I have it impending in me: grown heavy in my mind like a ripe pear; pendant, gravid, asking to be cut or it will fall.

Virginia Woolf

◆

I don't write easily or rapidly. My first draft usually has only a few elements worth keeping. I have to find what those are and build from them and throw out what doesn't work, or what simply is not alive.

Susan Sontag

◆

I write fairly rapidly if I get going, and don't change much, and have never been one for making outlines or taking out whole paragraphs or agonizing much. If a thing goes, it goes for me, and if it doesn't go, I eventually stop and get off.

John Updike

I don't write drafts. I do page one many, many times and move on to page two. I pile up sheet after sheet, each in its final state, and at length I have a novel that doesn't—in my view—need any revision.

Anthony Burgess

♦

I do a lot of revising. Certain chapters six or seven times. Occasionally you can hit it right the first time. More often, you don't.

John Dos Passos

♦

In composition, I do *not* think second thoughts are best.

Lord Byron

♦

I have rewritten—often several times—every word I have ever published. My pencils outlast their erasers.

Vladimir Nabokov

♦

Some poets actually say they don't revise, don't believe in revising. They say their originality suffers. I don't see that at all. The words that come first are anybody's, a froth of phrases, like the first words from a medium's mouth. You have to make them your own.

James Merrill

I never reread what I've written. I'm far too afraid to feel
ashamed of what I've done.

Jorge Luis Borges

♦

I never reread a text until I have finished the first draft. Otherwise it's too discouraging.

Gore Vidal

♦

The first draft of anything is shit.

Ernest Hemingway

♦

I work four hours a day and then usually early in the evening I read over what I've written during the day and I do a
lot of changing and shifting around. See, I write in longhand
and I do two versions of whatever I'm doing. I write first on
yellow paper and then I write on white paper and then when
I finally have it more or less settled the way I want, then I
type it. When I'm typing it, that's when I do my final rewrite.
I almost never change a word after that.

Truman Capote

I'll write a very rough first draft of every chapter, then I will rewrite every chapter. I try to get it down in the first rewrite, but some chapters I can't get quite right the third time. There are some I go over and over and over again.

Robert Stone

♦

I rise at first light and I start by rereading and editing everything I have written to the point I left off. That way I go through a book I'm writing several hundred times. Most writers slough off the toughest but most important part of their trade—editing their stuff, honing it and honing it until it gets an edge like a bullfighter's killing sword. One time my son Patrick brought me a story and asked me to edit it for him. I went over it carefully and changed one word. "But, Papa," he said, "you've only changed one word." I said: "If it's the right word, that's a lot."

Ernest Hemingway

♦

It takes me six months to do a story. I think it out and then write it sentence by sentence—no first draft. I can't write five words but that I change seven.

Dorothy Parker

I always write a story in one sitting.

Katherine Anne Porter

♦

What I do is try and write a slab of ten thousand words, and if it doesn't come off, I do it again.

Lawrence Durrell

♦

Each story tells me how to write *it*, but not the one afterwards.

Eudora Welty

♦

I revise the manuscript till I can't read it any longer, then I get somebody to type it. Then I revise the typing. Then it's retyped again. Then there's a third typing, which is the final one. Nothing should then remain that offends the eye.

Robert Graves

♦

Some authors type their works, but I cannot do that. Writing is tied up with the hand, almost with a special nerve.

Graham Greene

I write longhand and I type and I rewrite on the typed pages.
Joseph Heller

♦

I wrote in longhand at first, but I've lost it. I use two fingers on the typewriter.

Dorothy Parker

♦

I type in one place, but I write all over the house.
Toni Morrison

♦

The best time for planning a book is while you're doing the dishes.

Agatha Christie

♦

I always work on two things at a time. When one goes flat, I turn to the other.

Stephen Birmingham

♦

I never think when I write; nobody can do two things at the same time and do them well.

Don Marquis

I like to write when I feel spiteful; it's like having a good sneeze.

D.H. Lawrence

◆

I write slowly because I write badly. I have to rewrite everything many, many times just to achieve mediocrity.

William Gass

◆

I write fast because I have not the brains to write slow.

Georges Simenon

◆

I never "plan" a stanza. Words cluster like chromosomes, determining the procedure.

Marianne Moore

◆

I've always believed in writing without a collaborator, because where two people are writing the same book, each believes he gets all the worries and only half the royalties.

Agatha Christie

I never can understand how two men can write a book together; to me that's like three people getting together to have a baby.

Evelyn Waugh

♦

My method is to take the utmost trouble to find the right thing to say, and then to say it with the utmost levity.

George Bernard Shaw

♦

I talk out the lines as I write.

Tennessee Williams

♦

I always leave off the day before. As Thomas Mann advised, when the going is good, when you know exactly where you are and you are in a moment of exuberance, you stop. When I hook on the next morning, if the going was good I just go. I feel it emotionally, almost in the blood, the pulse, the excitement.

Marguerite Young

♦

The real writing process is simply sitting there and typing the same old lines over and over and over and over and sheet after sheet after sheet gets filled with the same shit.

William Gass

It's like making a movie: All sorts of accidental things will happen after you've set up the cameras. So you get lucky. Something will happen at the edge of the set and perhaps you start to go with that; you get some footage of that. You come into it accidentally. You set the story in motion, and as you're watching this thing begin, all these opportunities will show up.

Kurt Vonnegut

♦

We work in our own darkness a great deal with little real knowledge of what we are doing.

John Steinbeck

♦

When I'm near the end of the book, I sleep in the same room with it. Somehow the book doesn't leave you when you're asleep right next to it.

Joan Didion

♦

I don't know exactly how it's done. I let it alone a good deal.

Saul Bellow

Publicity

No writer, especially a young and unknown writer, resents publicity of any kind—whatever he may say.

Kingsley Amis

♦

If you write one book and then go on to another, readers pay half attention to the book and half attention to the publicity. Without publicity you lose the sense of an audience that has learned how to read you, or not. Everyone waits not so much for the book as for the essays and talk about the book.

Harold Brodkey

♦

I've had enough publicity to last an army of super rats. I don't know anybody who gets as much publicity as I do for doing nothing.

Truman Capote

Notoriety and public confession in literary form is a frazzler of the heart you were born with, believe me.

Jack Kerouac

♦

It's much more important to write than to be written about.

Gabriel García Márquez

♦

If a writer proclaims himself as isolated, uninfluenced and responsible to no one, he should not be surprised if he is ignored, uninfluential, and perceived as irresponsible.

Charles Newman

♦

It is very pleasant to be written up, even by a writer.

Joyce Cary

♦

A boy has to peddle his book.

Truman Capote

John Cheever

(1912–1982)

I once saw a woman on an elevator carrying a book of mine. She held the book backwards so I could see myself peering over her elbow. I found looking at myself very disconcerting and when she had left the elevator I had a terrible feeling that she was taking my face away with her, leaving me nothing to shave in the morning.

Publishers and Publishing

There are men that will make you books and turn 'em loose into the world with as much dispatch as they would do a dish of fritters.

Cervantes

♦

You write a book, you invest your imagination in it, and then you hand it over to a bunch of people who have no imagination and no understanding of their own enterprise.

Saul Bellow

♦

It circulated for five years, through the halls of fifteen publishers, and finally ended up with Vanguard Press, which, as you can see, is rather deep into the alphabet.

Patrick Dennis on Auntie Mame

It is with publishers as with wives: one always wants some-body else's.

Norman Douglas

◆

No author is a man of genius to his publisher.

Heinrich Heine

◆

A publisher who writes is like a cow in a milk bar.

Arthur Koestler

◆

Before publishers' blurbs were invented, authors had to make their reputations by writing.

Laurence J. Peter

◆

It is not wise to solicit the opinions of publishers—they be-come proud if you do.

Gore Vidal

I could show you all society poisoned by this class of person—a class unknown to the ancients—who, not being able to find any honest occupation, be it manual labor or service, and unluckily knowing how to read and write, become the brokers of literature, live on our works, steal our manuscripts, falsify them, and sell them.

Voltaire

♦

Publishers never tell writers anything. They're all crazy and they drive me crazy.

Anne Bernays

♦

Publishers are demons, there's no doubt about it.

William James

♦

As part of my research for *An Anthology of Authors' Atrocity Stories About Publishers*, I conducted a study (employing my usual controls) that showed the average shelf-life of a trade book to be somewhere between milk and yogurt. It is true that some books by Harold Robbins or any member of the Irving Wallace family last longer on the shelves, but they contain preservatives.

Calvin Trillin

Of course no writers ever forget their first acceptance. One fine day when I was seventeen I had my first, second and third, all in the same morning's mail. Oh, I'm here to tell you, dizzy with excitement is no mere phrase!

Truman Capote

♦

For several days after my first book was published I carried it about in my pocket, and took surreptitious peeps at it to make sure the ink had not faded.

James M. Barrie

♦

On the day the young writer corrects his first proof sheet he is as proud as a schoolboy who has just gotten his first dose of the pox.

Charles Baudelaire

♦

First publication is a pure, carnal leap into that dark which one dreams is life.

Hortense Calisher

♦

Literature is like any other trade; you will never sell anything unless you go to the right shop.

George Bernard Shaw

Publication is the auction of the Mind of Man.

Emily Dickinson

◆

I publish a piece in order to kill it, so that I won't have to fool around with it any longer.

William Gass

◆

In a very real sense, the writer writes in order to teach himself, to understand himself, to satisfy himself; the publishing of his ideas, though it brings gratifications, is a curious anticlimax.

Alfred Kazin

◆

During the final stages of publishing a paper or book, I always feel strongly repelled by my own writing...it appears increasingly hackneyed and banal and less worth publishing.

Konrad Lorenz

◆

A person who publishes a book willfully appears before the populace with his pants down.... If it is a good book nothing can hurt him. If it is a bad book, nothing can help him.

Edna St. Vincent Millay

Publication is a self-invasion of privacy.

Marshall McLuhan

♦

If you would be thrilled by watching the galloping advance of a major glacier, you'd be ecstatic watching changes in publishing.

John D. MacDonald

♦

The rules seem to be these: if you have written a successful novel, everyone invites you to write short stories. If you have written some good short stories, everyone wants you to write a novel. But nobody wants anything until you have already proved yourself by being published somewhere else.

James Michener

♦

Publishing is a very mysterious business. It is hard to predict what kind of sale or reception a book will have, and advertising seems to do very little good.

Thomas Wolfe

I think it is the most curious lack of judgment to publish before you are ready. If there are echoes of other people in your work, you're not ready. If anybody has to help you rewrite your story, you're not ready. A story should be a finished work before it is shown.

Katherine Anne Porter

♦

Manuscript: something submitted in haste and returned at leisure.

Oliver Herford

♦

Having been unpopular in high school is not just cause for book publication.

Fran Lebowitz

♦

If you do not write for publication, there is little point in writing at all.

George Bernard Shaw

♦

Nothing stinks like a pile of unpublished writing.

Sylvia Plath

I wonder whether what we are publishing now is worth cutting down trees to make paper for the stuff.

Richard Brautigan

♦

Publishing a volume of verse is like dropping a rose-petal down the Grand Canyon and waiting for the echo.

Don Marquis

Qualifications and Requirements

A writer needs three things, experience, observation and imagination, any two of which, at times any one of which, can supply the lack of the others.

William Faulkner

♦

Unprovided with original learning, unformed in the habits of thinking, unskilled in the arts of composition, I resolved to write a book.

Edward Gibbon

♦

The most essential gift for a good writer is a built-in shock-proof shit-detector.

Ernest Hemingway

To write fiction, one needs a whole series of inspirations about people in an actual environment, and then a whole lot of hard work on the basis of those inspirations.

Aldous Huxley

◆

How can you write if you can't cry?

Ring Lardner

◆

There is no need for the writer to eat a whole sheep to be able to tell what mutton tastes like. It is enough if he eats a cutlet.

W. Somerset Maugham

◆

The longer I live the more I become convinced that the only thing that matters in literature is the (more or less irrational) *shamantsvo* of a book, i.e., that the good writer is first of all an enchanter.

Vladimir Nabokov

◆

How vain it is to sit down to write when you have not stood up to live!

Henry David Thoreau

A writer doesn't need to go out and live, but stay home and invent.

Ned Rorem

♦

How can you know that something is worth writing about if you haven't seen anything else?

Paul Theroux

♦

It is necessary to remember and necessary to forget, but it is better for a writer to remember. It is necessary for him to live purposely, which is to say: to live and to remember having done so.

William Saroyan

♦

Real seriousness in regard to writing is one of the two absolute necessities. The other, unfortunately, is talent.

Ernest Hemingway

♦

The essential condition to become a creator in the artistic domain, particularly in the novel, is to be able to enter into the skin of people.

Georges Simenon

Henry James

(1843–1916)

I know everything. One has to, to write decently.

An absolutely necessary part of a writer's equipment, almost as necessary as talent, is the ability to stand up under punishment, both the punishment the world hands out and the punishment he inflicts upon himself.

Irwin Shaw

♦

A writer who does not passionately believe in the perfectibility of man has no dedication nor any membership in literature.

John Steinbeck

♦

A writer without a sense of justice and of injustice would be better off editing the Year Book of a school for exceptional children than writing novels.

Ernest Hemingway

♦

Context is all. And a relatively pure heart. *Relatively* pure—for if you had a pure heart you wouldn't be in the book-writing business in the first place.

Robert Penn Warren

Only a person who is congenitally self-centered has the effrontery and the stamina to write essays.

E.B. White

♦

To be a writer you need to see things as they are, and to see things as they are you need a certain basic innocence.

Tobias Wolff

♦

The one absolute requirement for me to write...is to be awake.

Isaac Asimov

♦

Writing doesn't require drive. It's like saying a chicken has to have drive to lay an egg.

John Updike

♦

All you need is a room without any particular interruptions.

John Dos Passos

♦

I need noise and interruptions and irritation: irritation and discomfort are a great starter. The loneliness of doing it any other way would kill me.

Anita Brookner

The actual process of writing. . .demands complete, noise-less privacy, without even music; a baby howling two blocks away will drive me nuts.

William Styron

♦

A woman must have money and a room of her own if she is to write fiction.

Virginia Woolf

♦

I like a room with a view, preferably a long view. I dislike looking out on gardens. I prefer looking at the sea, or ships, or anything which has a vista to it.

Norman Mailer

♦

The ideal view for daily writing, hour on hour, is the blank brick wall of a cold-storage warehouse. Failing this, a stretch of sky will do, cloudless if possible.

Edna Ferber

♦

A nice peaceful place with some good light.

Mary McCarthy

Quotation

Quoting: The act of repeating erroneously the words of another.

Ambrose Bierce

♦

I love quotations. I started keeping them when I was nineteen.

Louis L'Amour

♦

You could compile the worst book in the world entirely out of selected passages from the best writers in the world.

G.K. Chesterton

♦

When someone has the wit to coin a useful phrase, it ought to be acclaimed and broadcast or it will perish.

Jack Smith

Stay at home in your mind. Don't recite other people's opinions. I hate quotations. Tell me what you know.

Ralph Waldo Emerson

♦

I think we must quote whenever we feel that the allusion is interesting or helpful or amusing.

Clifton Fadiman

♦

To each reader those quotations are agreeable that neither strike him as hackneyed nor rebuke his ignorance.

H.W. Fowler

♦

It is the little writer rather than the great writer who seems never to quote, and the reason is that he is never really doing anything else.

Havelock Ellis

♦

The surest way to make a monkey of a man is to quote him.

Robert Benchley

♦

I quote others only the better to express myself.

Montaigne

I often quote myself. It adds spice to my conversation.

George Bernard Shaw

♦

Most anthologists...of quotations are like those who eat cherries...first picking the best ones and winding up by eating everything.

Nicolas Chamfort

Readers
and
Reading

He is so stupid you can't trust him with an idea.
He is so clever he will catch you in the least error.
He will not buy short books.
He will not buy long books.
He is part moron, part genius and part ogre.
There is some doubt as to whether he can read.

John Steinbeck

◆

No one can write decently who is distrustful of the reader's intelligence, or whose attitude is patronizing.

E.B. White

◆

The natural habit of any good and critical reader is to disbelieve what you are telling him and try to escape out of the world you are picturing.

Angus Wilson

Those who write clearly have readers; those who write obscurely have commentators.

Albert Camus

♦

Someone says, "Whom do you write for?" I reply: "Do you read me?" If they say, "Yes," I say, "Do you like it?" If they say, "No," then I say, "I don't write for you."

W.H. Auden

♦

I have no fans. You know what I got? Customers.

Mickey Spillane

♦

If there's one major cause for the spread of mass illiteracy, it's the fact that everybody can read and write.

Peter De Vries

♦

The ratio of literacy to illiteracy is constant, but nowadays the illiterates can read.

Alberto Moravia

♦

People don't like using dictionaries when they're reading mere novels.

Anthony Burgess

A great many people now reading and writing would be better employed keeping rabbits.

Edith Sitwell

♦

'Tis the good reader that makes the good book.

Ralph Waldo Emerson

♦

I think the writer ought to help the reader as much as he can without damaging what he wants to say; and I don't think it ever hurts the writer to sort of stand back now and then and look at his stuff as if he were reading it instead of writing it.

James Jones

♦

A writer's ambition should be to trade a hundred contemporary readers for ten readers in ten years' time and one reader in a hundred years' time.

Arthur Koestler

♦

I divide all readers into two classes; those who read to remember and those who read to forget.

William Lyon Phelps

There are some people who read too much: the bibliobibuli. I know some who are constantly drunk on books, as other men are drunk on whiskey or religion. They wander through this most diverting and stimulating of worlds in a haze, seeing nothing and hearing nothing.

H.L. Mencken

♦

An author ought to write for the youth of his own generation, the critics of the next, and the schoolmasters of ever afterward.

F. Scott Fitzgerald

♦

I don't have a sense of a so-called ideal reader and certainly not of a readership, that terrific entity. I write for the page.

Don DeLillo

♦

When I'm writing I'm always aware that this friend is going to like this, or that another friend is going to like that paragraph or chapter, always thinking of specific people. In the end all books are written for your friends.

Gabriel Garcia Márquez

I don't think I've ever written anything that is designed pure-
ly as a sop to the reader: I don't put in bits of sex to increase
sales. But I always bear him in mind, and try to visualize him
and watch for any signs of boredom or impatience to flit
across the face of this rather shadowy being, the Reader.

Kingsley Amis

♦

The ideal reader of my novels is a lapsed Catholic and failed
musician, shortsighted, color-blind, auditorily biased, who
has read the books that I have read. He should also be about
my age.

Anthony Burgess

♦

Every successful creative person creates with an audience
of one in mind.

Kurt Vonnegut

♦

Whenever I feel uneasy about my writing, I think: What
would be the response of the people in the book if they read
the book? That's my way of staying on track. Those are the
people for whom I write.

Toni Morrison

Flannery O'Connor

(1925–1964)

One old lady who wants her head lifted wouldn't be so bad, but you multiply her two hundred and fifty thousand times and what you get is a book club.

As in the sexual experience, there are never more than two persons present in the act of reading—the writer who is the impregnator, and the reader who is the respondent.

E.B. White

♦

When I write, I aim in my mind not toward New York but toward a vague spot a little to the east of Kansas. I think of the books on library shelves, without their jackets, years old, and a countryish teen-aged boy finding them, and having them speak to him. The reviews, the stacks in Brentano's, are just hurdles to get over, to place the books on that shelf.

John Updike

♦

I write for myself and strangers. The strangers, dear Readers, are an afterthought.

Gertrude Stein

♦

I don't think the artist should bother about his audience. His best audience is the person he sees in his shaving mirror every morning. I think that the audience an artist imagines, when he imagines that kind of thing, is a room filled with people wearing his own mask.

Vladimir Nabokov

There's only one person a writer should pay any attention to. It's not any damn critic. It's the reader.

William Styron

♦

The whole duty of a writer is to please and satisfy himself, and the true writer always plays to an audience of one.

E.B. White

♦

A man really writes for an audience of about ten persons. Of course, if others like it, that is clear gain. But if those ten are satisfied, he is content.

Alfred North Whitehead

♦

Your audience is one single reader. I have found that sometimes it helps to pick out one person—a real person you know, or an imagined person and write to that one.

John Steinbeck

♦

The greatest part of a writer's time is spent in reading, in order to write; a man will turn over half a library to make one book.

Samuel Johnson

Reading is a consolation, if not always an inspiration. It lessens the pain of the gratuitousness of writing.

Darryl Pinckney

♦

Magazines all too frequently lead to books and should be regarded by the prudent as the heavy petting of literature.

Fran Lebowitz

♦

I never desire to converse with a man who has written more books than he has read.

Samuel Johnson

♦

Easy reading is damned hard writing.

Nathaniel Hawthorne

Self-Criticism

Autocriticism does honor to the writer, dishonor to the critic.

Eugène Ionesco

◆

If there is a special hell for writers, it would be in the forced contemplation of their own works.

John Dos Passos

◆

I don't think many writers like their best-known piece of work, particularly when it was written a long time ago.

Lillian Hellman

If my books had been any worse I would not have been in-
vited to Hollywood, and if they had been any better I would
not have come.

Raymond Chandler

♦

I am always at a loss to know how much to believe of my
own stories.

Washington Irving

♦

The books I haven't written are better than the books other
people have.

Cyril Connolly

♦

I will not buy a magazine that will publish what I write.
Goodman Ace

♦

I'm a lousy writer; a helluva lot of people have got lousy taste.
Grace Metalious

$\mathscr{Style}$

Style is character. A good style cannot come from a bad, undisciplined character.

Norman Mailer

◆

The style is the man. Rather say the style is the way the man takes himself. It is with outer seriousness, it must be with inner humor. If it is with outer humor, it must be with inner seriousness.

Robert Frost

◆

Style is the physiognomy of the mind, and a safer index to character than the face.

Arthur Schopenhauer

Style is the hallmark of a temperament stamped upon the material at hand.

André Maurois

◆

Style is effectiveness of assertion.

George Bernard Shaw

◆

Proper words in proper places, make the true definition of a style.

Jonathan Swift

◆

Style is everything and nothing. It is not that, as is commonly supposed, you get your content and soup it up with style; style is absolutely embedded in the way you perceive.

Martin Amis

◆

One doesn't consider style, because style is.

Robert Stone

◆

Style is the mind skating circles round itself as it moves forward.

Robert Frost

I have no leisure to think of style or of polish, or to select the best language, the best English—no time to shine as an authoress. I must just think aloud, so as not to keep the public waiting.

Isabel Burton

♦

There is such an animal as a nonstylist, only they're not writers—they're typists.

Truman Capote

♦

I've been called a stylist until I really could tear my hair out. And I simply don't believe in style. The style is you.

Katherine Anne Porter

♦

Style has no fixed laws; it is changed by the usage of the people, never the same for any length of time.

Seneca

♦

What is written without effort is in general read without pleasure.

Samuel Johnson

As for style of writing, if one has anything to say, it drops from him simply and directly, as a stone falls to the ground.

Henry David Thoreau

◆

I am unlikely to trust a sentence that comes easily.

William Gass

◆

To write simply is as difficult as to be good.

W. Somerset Maugham

◆

You don't know what it is to stay a whole day with your head in your hands trying to squeeze your unfortunate brain so as to find a word.... Ah! I certainly know the agonies of style.

Gustave Flaubert

◆

You write with ease to show your breeding.
But easy writing's curst hard reading.

Richard Brinsley Sheridan

◆

All the fun's in how you say a thing.

Robert Frost

An author arrives at a good style when his language performs what is required of it without shyness.

Cyril Connolly

♦

If any man wishes to write in a clear style, let him first be clear in his thoughts.

Goethe

♦

A good style must, first of all, be clear. It must not be mean or above the dignity of the subject. It must be appropriate.

Aristotle

♦

Clear prose indicates the absence of thought.

Marshall McLuhan

♦

A good style should show no sign of effort. What is written should seem a happy accident.

W. Somerset Maugham

♦

No style is good that is not fit to be spoken or read aloud with effect.

William Hazlitt

Every style that is not boring is a good one.

Voltaire

◆

A strict and succinct style is that, where you can take away nothing without loss, and that loss to be manifest.

Ben Jonson

◆

The editorial "we" has often been fatal to rising genius; though all the world knows that it is only a form of speech, very often employed by a single needy blockhead.

Thomas Babington Macaulay

◆

Only presidents, editors and people with tapeworm have the right to use the editorial "we."

Mark Twain

◆

The greatest possible mint of style is to make the words absolutely disappear into the thought.

Nathaniel Hawthorne

◆

It takes less time to learn to write nobly than to learn to write lightly and straightforwardly.

Friedrich Wilhelm Nietzsche

We are surprised and delighted when we come upon a natural style, for instead of an author we find a man.

Blaise Pascal

♦

Literary people are forever judging the quality of the mind by the turn of expression.

Frank Moore Colby

♦

If the word *arse* is read in a sentence, no matter how beautiful the sentence, the reader will react only to that word.

Jules Renard

♦

I think of myself as a stylist, and stylists can become notoriously obsessed with the placing of a comma, the weight of a semicolon.

Truman Capote

♦

Anyone who can improve a sentence of mine by the omission or placing of a comma is looked upon as my dearest friend.

George Moore

All morning I worked on the proof of one of my poems, and I took out a comma; in the afternoon I put it back.

Oscar Wilde

♦

This morning I deleted the hyphen from "hell-hound" and made it one word; this afternoon I redivided it and restored the hyphen.

Edwin Arlington Robinson

♦

With sixty staring me in the face, I have developed inflammation of the sentence structure and a definite hardening of the paragraphs.

James Thurber

♦

A change of style is a change of subject.

Wallace Stevens

♦

Style comes only after long, hard practice and writing.

William Styron

Raymond Chandler
(1888–1959)

In the long run, however little you talk or even think about it, the most durable thing in writing is style, and style is the most valuable investment a writer can make with his time.

In stating as fully as I could how things really were, it was often very difficult and I wrote awkwardly and the awkwardness is what they called my style. All mistakes and awkwardness are easy to see, and they called it style.

Ernest Hemingway

◆

A story can be wrecked by a faulty rhythm in a sentence—especially if it occurs toward the end—or a mistake in paragraphing, even punctuation.

Truman Capote

◆

I am well aware that an addiction to silk underwear does not necessarily imply that one's feet are dirty. None the less, style, like sheer silk, too often hides eczema.

Albert Camus

◆

When I write after dark the shades of evening scatter their purple through my prose.

Cyril Connoly

Success

Success comes to a writer, as a rule, so gradually that it is always something of a shock to him to look back and realize the heights to which he has climbed.

P.G. Wodehouse

♦

As far as I can tell, the only healthy attitude for a writer is to consider praise, blame, book chat, and table position at Elaine's irrelevant to the writing, and to get on with it.

Jay McInerney

♦

Success is feminine and like a woman; if you cringe before her she will override you. So the way to treat her is to show her the back of your hand. Then maybe she will do the crawling.

William Faulkner

Literary success of any enduring kind is made by refusing to do what publishers want, by refusing to write what the public wants, by refusing to accept any popular standard, by refusing to write anything to order.

Lafcadio Hearn

♦

Success and failure are both difficult to endure. Along with success come drugs, divorce, fornication, bullying, travel, meditation, medication, depression, neurosis and suicide. With failure comes failure.

Joseph Heller

♦

In other countries, art and literature are left to a lot of shabby bums living in attics and feeding on booze and spaghetti, but in America the successful writer or picture-painter is indistinguishable from any other decent business man.

Sinclair Lewis

♦

The rarest thing in literature, and the only success, is when the author disappears and his work remains.

François Mauriac

If your first book is a smash, your second book gets kicked in the face.

John Berryman

◆

Failure is very difficult for a writer to bear, but very few can manage the shock of early success.

Maurice Valency

◆

Of all the enemies of literature, success is the most insidious.
Cyril Connolly

◆

Success and failure are equally disastrous.
Tennessee Williams

Talent

Talent, and genius as well, is like a grain of pearl sand shifting about in the creative mind. A valued tormentor.
Truman Capote

♦

Talent is like a faucet; while it is open, one must write. Inspiration is a farce that poets have invented to give themselves importance.

Jean Anouilh

♦

What can any of us do with this talent but try to develop his vision, so that through frequent failures we may learn better what we have missed in the past.
William Carlos Williams

There is no substitute for talent. Industry and all the virtues are of no avail.

Aldous Huxley

♦

Talent alone cannot make a writer. There must be a man behind the book.

Ralph Waldo Emerson

♦

Any writer, I suppose, feels that the world into which he was born is nothing less than a conspiracy against the cultivation of his talent—which attitude certainly has a great deal to support it. On the other hand, it is only because the world looks on his talent with such a frightening indifference that the artist is compelled to make his talent important.

James Baldwin

♦

I've put my genius into my life; I've only put my talent into my works.

Oscar Wilde

♦

Everyone has talent. What is rare is the courage to follow the talent to the dark place where it leads.

Erica Jong

We do not write as we want but as we can.

W. Somerset Maugham

◆

Talent is a matter of quantity: talent doesn't write one page, it writes three hundred.

Jules Renard

◆

Having no talent is no longer enough.

Gore Vidal

Talking About It

The writer must write what he has to say, not speak it.

Ernest Hemingway

♦

I have a superstition that if I talk about plot, it's like letting sand out of a hole in the bottom of a bag.

Shirley Hazzard

♦

I've never discussed my writing with others much, but I don't believe it can do any harm. I don't think that there's any risk that ideas or materials will evaporate.

Aldous Huxley

♦

Writers talk too much.

Lillian Hellman

Why do people always expect authors to answer questions?
I am an author because I want to *ask* questions. If I had an-
swers I'd be a politician.

Eugène Ionesco

♦

It is hard enough to write books and stories without being
asked to explain them as well.

Ernest Hemingway

♦

I just think it's bad to talk about one's present work, for it
spoils something at the root of the creative act. It discharges
the tension.

Norman Mailer

♦

The author should keep his mouth shut when his work begins to speak.

Friedrich Wilhelm Nietzsche

♦

Never talk about what you are going to do until after you
have written it.

Mario Puzo

Don't tell anybody what your book is about and don't show it until it's finished. It's not that anybody will steal your idea but that all that energy that goes into the writing of your story will be dissipated.

David Wallechinsky

♦

I don't like to talk about work-in-progress because if I do then it's on TV 10 weeks later, and it takes me two to three years to write a novel because I do so much rewriting.

Sidney Sheldon

♦

I don't care to talk about a novel I'm doing because if I communicate the magic spell, even in an abbreviated form, it loses its force for me. Once you have talked, the act of communication has been made.

Angus Wilson

♦

If the poem can be improved by its author's explanations, it never should have been published.

Archibald MacLeish

I don't like questions of explication. What did I mean by this
or that? I want the books to speak for themselves.

Bernard Malamud

♦

I really talk too much about my work and to anyone who
will listen. If I would limit my talk to inventions and keep
my big mouth shut about work, there would probably be
a good deal more work done.

John Steinbeck

♦

You lose it if you talk about it.

Ernest Hemingway

♦

I have never heard much that any writer has said about
writing that didn't embarrass me, including the things I say
about it.

John Barth

♦

You shouldn't pay very much attention to anything writers
say. They don't know why they do what they do. They're
like good tennis players or good painters, who are just full
of nonsense, pompous and embarrassing, or merely mistaken, when they open their mouths.

John Barth

Technique

Technique alone is never enough. You have to have passion. Technique alone is just an embroidered potholder.

Raymond Chandler

♦

Through the study of technique—not canoeing or logging or slinging hash—one learns the best, most efficient ways of making characters come alive, learns to know the difference between emotion and sentimentality, learns to discern, in the planning stages, the difference between the better dramatic action and the worse. It is this kind of knowledge... that leads to mastery. Mastery is not something that strikes in an instant, like a thunderbolt, but a gathering power that moves through time, like weather.

John Gardner

The language must be careful and must appear effortless.
It must not sweat. It must suggest and be provocative at the
same time.

Toni Morrison

♦

You lose energy and you gain technique.

Carlos Fuentes

♦

The best technique is none at all.

Henry Miller

♦

I don't know about method. The *what* is so much more important than how.

Ezra Pound

F. Scott Fitzgerald

(1896–1940)

All you can get from books is rhythm and technique.

Titles

A good title is the title of a successful book.

Raymond Chandler

♦

You'll find a title and it'll have a certain excitement for you; it will evoke the book, it will push you along. Eventually, you will use it up and you will have to choose another title. When you find the one that doesn't get used up, that's the title you go with.

E.L. Doctorow

♦

Titles distinguish the mediocre, embarrass the superior, and are disgraced by the inferior.

George Bernard Shaw

I have never been a title man. I don't give a damn what it is called.

John Steinbeck

◆

The title comes last.

Tennessee Williams

Tools

The tools I need for my work are paper, tobacco, food, and a little whiskey.

William Faulkner

♦

I believe more in the scissors than I do in the pencil.

Truman Capote

♦

Typewriter quotha!...I could never say what I would if I had to pick out my letters like a learned pig.

James Russell Lowell

♦

I believe that composing on the typewriter has probably done more than anything else to deteriorate English prose.

Edmund Wilson

The biggest obstacle to professional writing today is the necessity for changing a typewriter ribbon.

Robert Benchley

♦

I know so little about the typewriter that once I bought a new one because I couldn't change the ribbon on the one I had.

Dorothy Parker

♦

All I needed was a steady table and a typewriter. . .a marble-topped bedroom washstand table made a good place; the dining-room table between meals was also suitable.

Agatha Christie

♦

My schedule is flexible, but I am rather particular about my instruments: lined Bristol cards and well sharpened, not too hard, pencils capped with erasers.

Vladimir Nabokov

Pencils must be round. A hexagonal pencil cuts my fingers after a long day.

John Steinbeck

♦

The wastepaper basket is the writer's best friend.

Isaac Bashevis Singer

Words

Words are loaded pistols.

Jean-Paul Sartre

♦

Words are the supreme objects. They are *minded* things.
William Gass

♦

Words are...awkward instruments and they will be laid aside eventually, probably sooner than we think.
William Burroughs

♦

Words are an albatross to a writer—heavy, hopeless, fateful things. One writes to make words mean something new.
Joy Williams

Words have basic inalienable meanings, departure from which is either conscious metaphor or inexcusable vulgarity.

Evelyn Waugh

♦

Words are like leaves, and when they abound,
Much fruit of sense beneath is rarely found.

Alexander Pope

♦

Every word is like an unnecessary strain on silence and noth-ingness.

Samuel Beckett

♦

The difference between the right word and the almost right word is the difference between lightning and the light-ning bug.

Mark Twain

♦

For your born writer, nothing is so healing as the realiza-tion that he has come upon the right word.

Catherine Drinker Bowen

All my life I've looked at words as though I were seeing them for the first time.

Ernest Hemingway

◆

Why shouldn't we quarrel about a word? What is the good of words if they aren't important enough to quarrel over? Why do we choose one word more than another if there isn't any difference between them?

G.K. Chesterton

◆

You don't choose a word if you're a writer as a golf pro chooses a club with the *shot* in mind. You choose it with *yourself* in mind—*your* needs, *your* passions. It has to carry the green, yes, but it must also carry *you*.

Archibald MacLeish

◆

Words should be an intense pleasure to a writer just as leather should be to a shoemaker.

Evelyn Waugh

◆

Syllables govern the world.

John Selden

Words are like water—the assumption being that it moves in any direction.

Bernard Malamud

◆

There are too many words in prose, and they take up altogether too much room.

Edwin Arlington Robinson

◆

A writer lives in awe of words for they can be cruel or kind, and they can change their meanings right in front of you. They pick up flavors and odors like butter in a refrigerator.

John Steinbeck

◆

Words are all we have.

Samuel Beckett

Work Habits

It sounds shameful, but on my best days I write only about three or four hours.

Anne Bernays

♦

I find that in the course of the day when I'm writing, after three or four hours of intense work, I have a splitting headache, and I have to stop.

Edward Albee

♦

Thinking is the activity I love best, and writing to me is simply thinking through my fingers. I can write up to 18 hours a day. Typing 90 words a minute, I've done better than 50 pages a day. Nothing interferes with my concentration. You could put on an orgy in my office and I wouldn't look up—well, maybe once.

Isaac Asimov

I am a completely horizontal author. I can't think unless I'm lying down, either in bed or stretched on a couch and with a cigarette and coffee handy. I've got to be puffing and sipping. As the afternoon wears on, I shift from coffee to mint tea to sherry to martinis.

Truman Capote

♦

I work mornings only. I go out to lunch. Afternoons I play with the baby, walk with my husband, or shovel mail.

Annie Dillard

♦

The best regimen is to get up early, insult yourself a bit in the shaving mirror, and then pretend you're cutting wood.

Lawrence Durrell

♦

A man may write at any time, if he will set himself doggedly to it.

Samuel Johnson

♦

When my horse is running good, I don't stop to give him sugar.

William Faulkner

I write when I feel like it and wherever I feel like it, and I feel like it most of the time.

Jerzy Kosinski

♦

I generally go to work right after breakfast. I sit right down to the machine. If I find I'm not able to write, I quit.

Henry Miller

♦

After I get up it takes me an hour and a half of fiddling around before I can get up the courage and nerve to go to work. I smoke half a pack of cigarettes, drink six or seven cups of coffee, read over what I wrote the day before. Finally there's no further excuse. I go to the typewriter. Four to six hours of it. Then I quit and we go out. Or stay home and read.

James Jones

♦

I prefer to get up very early in the morning and work. I don't want to speak to anybody or see anybody. Perfect silence. I work until the vein is out.

Katherine Anne Porter

The desk in the room, near the bed, with a good light, midnight till dawn, a drink when you get tired, preferably at home, but if you have no home, make a home out of your hotel room or motel room or pad: peace.

Jack Kerouac

♦

I work every day—or at least I force myself into office or room. I may get nothing done, but you don't earn bonuses without putting in time. Nothing may come for three months, but you don't earn the fourth without it.

Mordecai Richler

♦

I work every day, from ten in the morning till I'm done with my pages. I try not to write beyond a certain point. It's my experience that if I write too much in one day it kills a couple of days' work for me after that. I like to keep myself to three or four pages a day.

Scott Spencer

♦

I start early in the morning. I'm usually out in the woods with the dog as soon as it gets light; then I drink a whole lot of tea and start as early as I can, and I go as long as I can.

Robert Stone

I used to start at eight and stop at maybe three or four. Now I start at nine or ten and hopefully stop at four or five. Every day I write. If there is ever an interruption, like an electric-meter man or a doorbell ringing, it drives me crazy. I don't care how many people call me up, but I don't want anyone near me physically. I don't want to see anyone. I'm just absolutely closed in, and I get more so as the years go by, more and more loving of privacy.

Marguerite Young

♦

I work whenever I'm let.

Katherine Anne Porter

♦

First coffee. Then a bowel movement. Then the muse joins me.

Gore Vidal

♦

I find it easier to get up early in the morning, and I like to get through by one or two o'clock. I don't do very much in the afternoon. I like to get out of doors then if I can.

John Dos Passos

I usually write to a point where the work is getting worse rather than better. That's the point to stop and the time to publish.

John Dos Passos

♦

You write by sitting down and writing. There's no particular time or place—you suit yourself, your nature. How one works, assuming he's disciplined, doesn't matter.

Bernard Malamud

♦

I write whenever it suits me. During a creative period I write every day; a novel should not be interrupted. When I cease to be carried along, when I no longer feel as though I were taking down dictation, I stop.

François Mauriac

♦

My usual method...is to spend the mornings turning over the text in my mind. Then in the afternoon, between two and five, I call in a secretary and dictate to her. I can do about two thousand words. It took me about ten years to learn.

James Thurber

I put a piece of paper under my pillow, and when I could not sleep I wrote in the dark.

Henry David Thoreau

♦

I never quite know when I'm not writing. Sometimes my wife comes up to me at a party and says, "Dammit, Thurber, stop writing." She usually catches me in the middle of a paragraph.

James Thurber

♦

I deemed it expedient to bind myself to certain self-imposed laws. It was also my practice to allow myself no mercy.

Anthony Trollope

♦

I write every weekday morning.

John Updike

♦

I like to stay up late at night and get drunk and sleep late. I wish I could break the habit but I can't. The afternoon is the only time I have left and I try to use it to the best advantage, with a hangover.

William Styron

I need an hour alone before dinner, with a drink, to go over what I've done that day. I can't do it late in the afternoon because I'm too close to it. Also, the drink helps. It removes me from the pages.

Joan Didion

♦

There comes a moment in the day, when you have written your pages in the morning, attended to your correspondence in the afternoon, and have nothing further to do. Then comes the hour when you are bored; that's the time for sex.

H.G. Wells

♦

When I stop [working], the rest of the day is posthumous. I'm only really alive when I'm working.

Tennessee Williams

Writer's Block

I've never been big on the agony of writing. I see no evidence that Tolstoy suffered from writer's block.

James Michener

♦

When I feel difficulty coming on, I switch to another book I'm writing. When I get back to the problem, my unconscious has solved it.

Isaac Asimov

♦

When I have trouble writing, I step outside my studio into the garden and pull weeds until my mind clears—I find weeding to be the best therapy there is for writer's block.

Irving Stone

American writers drink a lot when they're "blocked" and drunkenness—being a kind of substitute for art—makes the block worse.

Anthony Burgess

♦

The successful writer listens to himself. You get a writer's block by being aware that you're putting it out there.

Frank Herbert

♦

It has been said that writing comes more easily if you have something to say.

Sholem Asch

♦

Writers are notorious for using any reason to keep from working: over-researching, retyping, going to meetings, waxing the floors—anything.

Gloria Steinem

♦

I don't get writing blocks except from the stationer, but I do feel so sickened by what I write that I don't want to go on.

Anthony Burgess

There is always a point in the writing of a piece when I sit in a room literally papered with false starts and cannot put one word after another and imagine that I have suffered a small stroke, leaving me apparently undamaged but actually aphasic.

Joan Didion

♦

I went for years not finishing anything. Because, of course, when you finish something you can be judged.... I had poems which were rewritten so many times I suspect it was just a way of avoiding sending them out.

Erica Jong

♦

The hardest thing for a writer to decide is whether he's burned out or merely lying fallow.

Norman Mailer

♦

Every writer I know has trouble writing.

Joseph Heller

Writers and Writing

The writer. . . is a person who talks to himself, or better, who talks in himself.

Malcolm Cowley

◆

The writer is the Faust of modern society, the only surviving individualist in a mass age. To his orthodox contemporaries he seems a semi-madman.

Boris Pasternak

◆

A writer is someone who always sells. An author is one who writes a book that makes a big splash.

Mickey Spillane

A writer is not someone who expresses his thoughts, his passion or his imagination in sentences but someone who thinks sentences. A Sentence-Thinker.

Roland Barthes

♦

I think you must remember that a writer is a simple-minded person to begin with and go on that basis. He's not a great mind, he's not a great thinker, he's not a great philosopher, he's a storyteller.

Erskine Caldwell

♦

There is only one trait that marks the writer. He is always watching. It's a kind of trick of mind and he is born with it.

Morley Callaghan

♦

The role of the writer is not to say what we can all say, but what we are unable to say.

Anaïs Nin

♦

Writers are always selling somebody out.

Joan Didion

Most writers are in a state of gloom a good deal of the time; they need perpetual reassurance.

John Hall Wheelock

♦

Writers, like teeth, are divided into incisors and grinders.

Walter Bagehot

♦

A writer's mind seems to be situated partly in the solar plexus and partly in the head.

Ethel Wilson

♦

The true function of a writer is to produce a masterpiece and...no other task is of any consequence.

Cyril Connolly

♦

Writers can treat their mental illnesses every day.

Kurt Vonnegut

♦

Writers shouldn't propound their own theories. They should do what painters do: Get their wives, husbands, or old school chums to write the manifestoes.

Tom Wolfe

H. L. Mencken

(1880–1956)

A bad writer has no rights whatever. Any mercy shown to him is wasted and mistaken.

There is no way of being a creative writer in America without being a loser.

Nelson Algren

◆

Our society, like decadent Rome, has turned into an amusement society, with writers chief among the court jesters—not so much above the clatter as part of it.

Saul Bellow

◆

American writers never have a second act.

F. Scott Fitzgerald

◆

In America only the successful writer is important, in France all writers are important, in England no writer is important, in Australia you have to explain what a writer is.

Geoffrey Cotterell

◆

Whenever citizens are seen routinely as enemies of their own government, writers are routinely seen to be the most dangerous enemies.

E.L. Doctorow

The writer, like the priest, must be exempted from secular labor. His work needs a frolic health; he must be at the top of his condition.

Ralph Waldo Emerson

◆

Everything goes by the board: honor, pride, decency. . .to get the book written. If a writer has to rob his mother, he will not hesitate; the "Ode on a Grecian Urn" is worth any number of old ladies.

William Faulkner

◆

No wonder the really powerful men in our society, whether politicians or scientists, hold writers and poets in contempt. They do it because they get no evidence from modern literature that anybody is thinking about any significant question.

Saul Bellow

◆

I am convinced that all writers are optimists whether they concede the point or not. . . . How otherwise could any human being sit down to a pile of blank sheets and decide to write, say two hundred thousand words on a given theme?

Thomas Costain

There are other writers who would persuade you not to go on, that everything is nonsense, that you should kill yourself. They, of course, go on to write another book while you have killed yourself.

John Gardner

◆

Writers are interesting people, but often mean and petty.
Lillian Hellman

◆

Many people who want to be writers don't really want to be writers. They want to *have been* writers. They wish they had a book in print.

James Michener

◆

Good writers are monotonous, like good composers. Their truth is self-repeating.... They keep trying to perfect their understanding of the one problem they were born to understand.

Alberto Moravia

◆

What I like in a good author is not what he says, but what he whispers.

Logan Pearsall Smith

A great writer creates a world of his own and his readers are proud to live in it. A lesser writer may entice them in for a moment, but soon he will watch them filing out.

Cyril Connolly

♦

Great writers are always evil influences; second-rate writers are not wicked enough to become great.

George Bernard Shaw

♦

Screenwriters are like little gypsies swimming in an aquarium filled with sharks, killer whales, squid, octopuses and other creatures of the deep. And plenty of squid shit.

Joseph Wambaugh

♦

We romantic writers are there to make people feel and not think.

Barbara Cartland

♦

When one says that a writer is fashionable one practically always means that he is admired by people under thirty.

George Orwell

He is a writer for the ages—the ages of four to eight.

Dorothy Parker

♦

Why has the South produced so many good writers? Because we got beat.

Walker Percy

♦

When I'm asked why Southern writers particularly have a penchant for writing about freaks, I say it's because we are still able to recognize one.

Flannery O'Connor

♦

Being a writer in the South has its special miseries, which include isolation, madness, tics, amnesia, alcoholism, lust, and loss of ordinary powers of speech. One may go for days without saying a word.

Walker Percy

♦

What no wife of a writer can ever understand is that a writer is working when he's staring out the window.

Burton Rascoe

If, as Dr. Johnson said, a man who is not married is only half a man, so a man who is very much married is only half a writer.

Cyril Connolly

◆

Pretty women swarm around everybody but writers. Plain, intelligent women *somewhat,* swarm around writers.

William Saroyan

◆

Writers age more quickly than athletes.

Tennessee Williams

◆

A writer has nothing to say after the age of forty; if he is clever he knows how to hide it.

Georges Simenon

◆

If you're a singer, you lose your voice. A baseball player loses his arm. A writer gets more knowledge, and if he's good, the older he gets, the better he writes.

Mickey Spillane

I am more interested in works than in authors.

E.M. Forster

♦

I get very tired of reading about writers. I don't even understand why people want to read novels about them. There's apparently some glamour, but I'll be damned if I can see it. I would much rather try to understand the lives of people who don't write letters to the *New York Review of Books.*

Rosellen Brown

♦

The best part of every author is in general to be found in his book, I assure you.

Samuel Johnson

♦

The life of a writer has always seemed to me to be about as good a one as a low human being could hope for.

George Jean Nathan

♦

Writers...live over-strained lives in which far too much humanity is sacrificed to far too little art.

Raymond Chandler

There is no denying the fact that writers should be read but not seen. Rarely are they a winsome sight.

Edna Ferber

♦

You shouldn't pay very much attention to anything writers say. They don't know why they do what they do. They're like good tennis players or good painters, who are just full of nonsense, pompous and embarrassing, or merely mistaken, when they open their mouths.

John Barth

♦

Most writers...are awful sticks to talk with.

Sherwood Anderson

♦

No complete son of a bitch ever wrote a good sentence.

Malcolm Cowley

♦

Every asshole in the world wants to write.

Judith Rossner

Never believe anything a writer tells you about himself. A man comes to believe in the end the lies he tells himself about himself.

George Bernard Shaw

♦

We are all apprentices in a craft where no one ever becomes a master.

Ernest Hemingway

♦

Writing is turning one's worst moments into money.

J.P. Donleavy

♦

Writing is a form of self-flagellation.

William Styron

♦

Writing is a struggle against silence.

Carlos Fuentes

♦

Writing is busy idleness.

Goethe

All writing is pigshit. People who come out of nowhere to try to put into words any part of what goes on in their minds are pigs.

Antonin Artaud

♦

Writing is: the science of the various blisses of language.
Roland Barthes

♦

Writing is a dog's life, but the only life worth living.
Gustave Flaubert

♦

Writing's not terrible, it's wonderful. I keep my own hours, do what I please. When I want to travel, I can. But mainly I'm doing what I most wanted to do all my life. I'm not into the agonies of creation.

Raymond Carver

♦

I love being a writer. What I can't stand is the paperwork.
Peter De Vries

The desire to write grows with writing.

Erasmus

♦

Anything that isn't writing is easy.

Jimmy Breslin

♦

To practice art in order to earn money, flatter the public, spin facetious or dismal yarns for reputation or cash—that is the most ignoble of professions.

Gustave Flaubert

♦

Writing is a yoga that invokes Lord mind.

Allen Ginsberg

♦

Writing is making sense of life.

Nadine Gordimer

♦

Writing is putting one's obsessions in order.

Jean Grenier

Writing is a suspension of life in order to re-create life.

John McPhee

♦

Writing is the hardest work in the world not involving heavy lifting.

Pete Hamill

♦

Writing is one of the few professions left where you take all the responsibility for what you do. It's really dangerous and ultimately destroys you as a writer if you start thinking about responses to your work or what your audience needs.

Erica Jong

♦

Writing is no trouble: you just jot down ideas as they occur to you. The jotting is simplicity itself—it is the occurring which is difficult.

Stephen Leacock

♦

To write is to inform against others.

Violette Leduc

I love writing. I love the swirl and swing of words as they tangle with human emotions.

James Michener

♦

Writing, like life itself, is a voyage of discovery.

Henry Miller

♦

Writing doesn't get easier with experience. The more you know, the harder it is to write.

Tim O'Brien

♦

You can recover from the writing malady only by falling mortally ill and dying.

Jules Renard

♦

Writing is just having a sheet of paper, a pen and not a shadow of an idea of what you're going to say.

Françoise Sagan

Gustave Flaubert

(1821–1880)

It is splendid to be a great writer, to put men into the frying pan of your imagination and make them pop like chestnuts.

When I stepped from hard manual work to writing, I just stepped from one kind of hard work to another.

Sean O'Casey

◆

To me, writing is a horseback ride into heaven and hell and back. I am grateful if I can crawl back alive.

Thomas Sanchez

◆

The great art of writing is the art of making people real to themselves with words.

Logan Pearsall Smith

◆

The craft or art of writing is the clumsy attempt to find symbols for the wordlessness. In utter loneliness a writer tries to explain the inexplicable.

John Steinbeck

◆

Great writing has been a staff to lean on, a mother to consult, a wisdom to pick up stumbling folly, a strength in weakness and a courage to support sick cowardice.

John Steinbeck

Writing...keeps me from believing everything I read.

Gloria Steinem

♦

For me, writing is the only thing that passes the three tests of *métier*: (1) when I'm doing it, I don't feel that I should be doing something else instead; (2) it produces a sense of accomplishment and, once in a while, pride; and (3) it's frightening.

Gloria Steinem

♦

Writing, when properly managed (as you may be sure I think mine is), is but a different name for conversation.

Laurence Sterne

♦

This is what I find most encouraging about the writing trades: They allow mediocre people who are patient and industrious to revise their stupidity, to edit themselves into something like intelligence. They also allow lunatics to seem saner than sane.

Kurt Vonnegut

What is wrong with most writing today is its flaccidity, its lack of pleasure in the manipulation of sounds and pauses. The written word is becoming inert. One dreads to think what it will be like in 2020.

Anthony Burgess

◆

The purpose of writing is to hold a mirror to nature, but too much today is written from small mirrors in vanity cases.

John Mason Brown

◆

All writing is communication; creative writing is communication through revelation—it is the self escaping into the open. No writer long remains incognito.

E.B. White

◆

Incessant scribbling is death to thought.

Thomas Carlyle

◆

Writers don't have lifestyles. They sit in little rooms and write.

Norman Mailer

I think the whole glory of writing lies in the fact that it forces us out of ourselves and into the lives of others.

Sherwood Anderson

♦

This sickness, to express oneself. What is it?

Jean Cocteau

Index
of
Writers

Index